TALES
and
TRADITIONS
of
OLD TENBY

Alison Bielski © 1979

Based on "Tales and Traditions of Tenby", published and printed by Richard Mason, High Street, Tenby, and also by Piper, Stephenson and Spence, Paternoster Row, London, in 1858.
With added material from other sources.

First Impression, 1981

SBN: 901906 17 4

PRINTED IN WALES BY
THE FIVE ARCHES PRESS,
TENBY, DYFED.

for
Ronald, Maggie, Helen
and my grandchildren
in the hope that they
may help to keep
these traditions alive

Acknowledgements

I would like to express my thanks to all my friends and colleagues in Pembrokeshire and Gwent, who have helped me to produce this book, and I would especially mention the following who have shown so much interest and given me valuable assistance and contributions of local material:

Mr. H. H. B. Lee; Lt. Col. F. Day; Archdeacon I. Phillips; Mr. D. C. Rhys Jones; the Tenby Museum for use of its facilities; Miss V. Allen and Staff of Tenby Library; Mr. A. R. Edwards and the Staff of Haverfordwest County Library; Staff of Newport, Gwent, Reference Library; Tenby Arts Club, for their encouragement and understanding; Mr. A. W. Haggar of South Pembs. District Council, for supplying details of the Harbour Act; Mr. Anthony Conran for his permission to reproduce his translation "Praise of Tenby", printed in The Penguin Book of Welsh Verse. © A. Conran; Miss S. Hollingdrake of Newport, Gwent; Mr. and Mrs. I. Crockford and their family; Mrs. M. Crockford and her family; Mr. and Mrs. K. Shaw; Mr. Gareth Walters for his patience and assistance; Miss Helen Bielski, my daughter, for her support while I prepared and typed the manuscript.

Contents

1 Pirates
2 Smugglers
3 Sea-Dogs and Privateers
4 Wrecks
5 The Tenby Lifeboat
6 Temperament and Way of Life
7 Courting, a Welsh Bidding, The Ceffyl Prên
8 Birth and Death
9 Ghosts, the "Little Fair Folk", Charmers and Witches
10 Seasonal Customs. 1 Christmas
11 Seasonal Customs. 2 New Year and Twelfth Night
12 Seasonal Customs. 3 Easter and Whitsun
13 Seasonal Customs. 4 Harvest and Hallowe'en
14 The Sea Serjeants - A Secret Society
15 Old Tenby, the Market and St. Margaret's Fair
16 The Harbour
17 Buildings of Tenby
18 The Escape of Henry VII from Tenby, the French Invasion, the Gunfort
19 Visitors and Benefactors
20 Caldey Island and St. Margaret's
21 Penally and St. Florence
22 Personalities
23 Exhibits, Shells and Collectors

1

Pirates

Paul Jones, the pirate, was called the scourge of the British coasts at the end of the eighteenth century. On his way to Waterwynch Bay, between Saundersfoot and Tenby, he was in the habit of watering on Caldey Island, where the water supply was excellent, and where he was hidden from the Tenby coastguard at the back of the island. (Archaeologia Cambrensis 1908).

He was said to be a man of tenacious courage and an excellent seaman. He became an Admiral in the United States Navy and was a hero of Great Britain and America at the age of thirty-three. He died in 1792 at the age of forty-five. Referring to Trafalgar in 1805, Napoleon said that Lord Nelson might have found in him a worthy antagonist.

Richard Mason, in "Tales and Traditions of Tenby", gives an account of Paul Jones' visit to Tenby, where he was well liked, under the heading "The Suspicious Stranger", and Mr. and Mrs. S.C. Hall give the following account of the same incident:

"Many years ago, the town was thrown into a state of agitation by the report that a very suspicious looking craft had anchored in Caldy Roads, having every appearance of a vessel of war, only that she had no guns visible. As the day wore on, curiosity had brought almost the whole population down to anywhere from whence a sight of her could be obtained.

"A boat was sent off to learn what she was, but the account she gave not being satisfactory, a council was held, and it was settled to fire upon her.

A gun was brought up and planted on the cliff, but not a shot struck. At last, some of them thought of sending for an old man-of-war's man, who went down loaded, brought the gun to bear, and fired. The first shot sent the spray over the bulwarks of the ship; the second knocked away her fore-top mast.

"Before the cheer that greeted the sailor had died away, a respectable looking gentleman, dressed in black, with a riding-whip in his hand, who had been looking on, touched him on the shoulder, and exclaimed:

"'Bravo, my man - a capital shot that last; it deserves a glass of brandy - does it not my friends?', he asked, turning to those who crowded round.

"All were of one opinion and they adjourned to a tavern; the result was - not another shot was fired.

"Towards nightfall, the gentleman who had behaved so liberally engaged a boat and crew to pull him out to a brig that was seen crossing the horizon towards the English coast. The boatmen at first refused to go, but on being promised a good sum of money, their hesitation vanished. As they reached the Woolhouse Rocks, the stranger who was sitting in the bow with a glass in his hand scanning the horizon suddenly turned round and cried out 'helm-a-port, quick!'

"'Why, that will bring us right on the ship in the roads'', urged the man who was steering.

"'Precisely so; 'tis there I wish to go', was the reply of the passenger, as he pulled out a brace of pistols, and pointed them at the men's heads; "and harkee! if you don't immediately do as I command, I will shoot two of you, and pitch the other overboard'.

"The men were obliged to obey, and when they reached the ship they found her ready for sea, with the mast neatly repaired. An hour afterwards, when they left, having received what had been agreed upon, and as much brandy as they could drink, the stranger wished them good-bye, and requested them to inform the people of Tenby how they had been treated by Paul Jones!"

The object in making the boatmen drunk must have been to prevent their return to Tenby to give the alarm before he had succeeded in discharging his cargo.

One of Paul Jones' men was called "Leekie Porridge" and was a native of Tenby. The sailors there used to sing a song, one verse of which ran thus:-

"It's of an American frigate, a ship of great fame,
Mounting guns forty-four, from New York she came,
For to cruise in the Channel of old England of great fame,
With a noted commander, Paul Jones was his name".

After Paul Jones' disappearance from these waters, Leekie Porridge returned home, acting as a pilot. One day, going on board a ship in the bay, the captain recognised him as one of Paul Jones' men. The captain came in to Tenby and informed upon him before the magistrates. Leekie Porridge was arrested and tried, "the captain proving him to have been with Paul Jones and further that the silver buckles he then wore in his shoes were his (the captain's) property, having been taken from him when his vessel was plundered by the pirates"!

He was convicted of this offence and sentenced to be sent on board a man-of-war where he was, "owing to a scarcity of men, replaced in his former situation of a quarter-master, from which office he had formerly deserted to join Paul Jones. He served in the navy until peace was proclaimed, when he again returned to Tenby".

Turkish pirates also were said to infest the coasts of north-western Europe. The Ulster Journal of Archaeology for 1855 says that "it is most probable that these pirates were not Turks, but Algerines."

The reader of Camden will find a reference to one "William de Marisco, a mischievous Pirat, who from hence (i.e. Lundy, opposite Caldy) infested these coasts in the reign of Henry III."

In the fourteenth century, an enquiry was made by Simon de Burley and James Lyons, sergeant-at-arms, who had received information that the inhabitants of Tenby "had seized a great ship of Genoa laden with two barrels of gold plate and other merchandise" and had removed the cargo to the town.

There is a very long poem about a pirate called "The Spectre Ship and Pirate Chief", quoted in Mason's "Tales and Traditions of Tenby", the story of which is as follows:

One winter evening in about 1558, the reign of Queen Elizabeth I, a vessel swept across Carmarthen Bay, which seemed to be empty, but watchers described lights and spirit-forms upon the deck, as she sank into the sand. Strange sounds were heard all night, but in the morning, when the storm had calmed, no trace of the ship could be found. Upon the shore lay a man, wearing strange clothes, in a deep sleep.

He would not live among the local people, but spent his time on St. Catherine's Island. One day a shepherd, missing the familiar figure, went to the Island with food and clothes. He often, after that first visit, found him sitting there on a crag with the wild seabirds around him. The shepherd begged the man to go home with him, but the stranger refused courteously. He then talked of his former life as a pirate, and also said that, in a fit of jealousy, he had killed the one who loved him most. All his comrades had perished on his ship, which was then manned by spirit-forms and wrecked upon that coast.

At times, he said, sea maidens came and beckoned him into the sea.

They told him that his girl was happy and at rest. Suddenly, he pointed to a white wave, crying out "I come. I come. Receive me, spirits blest!", and sprang into the waves, drowning immediately. The horrified shepherd watched, but saw no trace of the man and went home alone.

St. Catherines Island

2

Smugglers

Smuggling was widely carried on along the Pembrokeshire coast, and Revenue cutters were always on the look-out for illegal trading.

One smuggler escaped from such a cutter over the ridge of rocks that connects the islands of Caldey and St. Margarets. Due to a rise in the rock level, boats today avoid this dangerous reef.

From a survey taken in the summer of 1856, in the bay opposite the vale of St. Florence, it was discovered that the rocks were two foot nearer the surface than in the previous survey eighteen years before. Several of the old sailors maintained that rocks had "grown nearer the surface, and instance one near the western part of St. Margaret's Island which was formerly safe to pass over even at the lowest tides, but now it has risen so high that recently a boat was capsized upon it". This change of level was said to have taken place only upon carboniferous limestone, not affecting the adjacent coal measures in the area.

On the Marsh road outside Tenby, late one night, an excise officer met a man and his son bringing two kegs of brandy into the town. These were slung across a horse's back. The exciseman called for help and managed to bring them into Tenby, where he left the brandy inside the door of his own house in St. Julian Street. He then went to put the horse in the stable of the Anchor, which is now the Cobourg Hotel.

While he was away, the smugglers opened the door of the house and took away the kegs of brandy to their destination. They then took their horse out of the Anchor stable and got safely away!

A tale was told by William Cadwallader, the landlord of the Union Tavern in Tenby, of how in Napoleon's time a Mr.– came over from Cornwall to Tenby, staying there until he took over the Park Farm at Manorbier, where the castle stands. William then went to Manorbier and was employed by this man, together with five Cornish men known by the nicknames of Blue Boy, Jack Strong, The Long-un, Little Dick and Jack Tar.

They landed many cargoes at Manorbier and sometimes one at Lydstep, bringing the kegs over in carts, if the surf was too great at Manorbier, owing to bad weather. One boat turned over when it was coming ashore, throwing kegs and men into the water. At least seventy men were in the sea, but everything was saved. It was usual practice, when landing a cargo, for a keg to be placed on its end, the head knocked in and a cup placed by the side of it for everyone to help themselves. The father of the storyteller had to be carried home, having had too much to drink.

Cellars had been dug all over the cliffs, two on Hill Farm, two under the old parsonage walls by Manorbier Church, two outside the castle walls, but the greatest quantity of kegs was stored under the castle itself.

These spirits were brought by ships from Jersey, which peddled along the coast. At Manorbier they took about 200 to 500 kegs of eight gallons each, which was sold at ten shillings per gallon, old wine measure. This was brandy, rum or "hollands" (gin). Mr. Cadwallader's master had shares in several vessels, and it was believed a lieutenant in the Royal Navy had one also. The ships usually got away safely, but the smuggling cutter, Jane, with Captain Furze, had a narrow escape.

Only six men knew the location of these cellars, and although sometimes eighty people would help with the unloading, they only carried the kegs to a certain place for collection and storage by those in the know.

If it was not possible to land all the cargo, the kegs would be strung together with a rope weighted with stones, and with a grapnel attached to each end to prevent drifting, which kept the kegs safe until they could be landed.

In one spring tide with a heavy gale, twenty-eight kegs were washed up, which had been buried in sand below the castle. William Cadwallader was bringing a keg ashore when he heard the warning voices of their men and, looking round, he saw the Custom House officers close at hand. He ran along the cliffs towards Tenby, passed Cwm's Quoit, the cromlech, crossed the fissures, climbed over a stone wall and did not come back until the night, when he found the beach covered with people. The village women helped to carry away some of the kegs, but most of this cargo was lost.

One morning, when he was returning from snipe shooting, he saw the King's lugger, the Stag, with Captain Hopkins in the bay, and a boat coming ashore. The men landed and searched the castle, discovering one of the main cellars which was most frequently used. This cellar had been made inside the castle by sinking a small shaft down some twelve feet from the surface. At the bottom, the cellar branched off at a right angle, while the top of the shaft was covered with a large stone, having a ring in the centre. This was placed about six inches below the surface and covered with soil, then turf. Unfortunately, this turf had curled up because of frost that morning, and so betrayed their hiding-place.

William Cadwallader's master now suffered very heavy losses and, after they had been betrayed again, Lord Cawdor seized 300 kegs of spirits, as well as tea, tobacco and silk, most of which had been deposited on the top of the round tower, at the angle of the castle near the entrance next to the Church. The master left, breaking up the establishment and dismissing all but one servant. After this, it is said that there was no further smuggling at Manorbier, but some transactions were said to have been carried on at Swanlake.

Another smuggling account was given to Richard Mason by a housewife, who lived in one of the villagers' cottages in Manorbier. This is quoted in her own words:

"At about noon one hot Saturday in the summer of 1825, a woman of Swanlake came up to me, carrying a fine girl in her arms. I said 'Mary, where are you going so fast, and with such a load?'

"'Oh,' says she 'Lewis (her husband) and me have been left in charge of a cargo of smuggled spirits, which was landed on Thursday night, and we have agreed to inform, and get the reward, which on this large quantity cannot be less than £200, and that, you know, would be a great thing for us, so goodbye, I cannot stay any longer.'

"Immediately she left, I put on my bonnet and ran to Mr. J... of Pembroke, and found his wife in the kitchen.

'Where is J...?'

'Oh! he is in the garden'.

'Then let me see him immediately.'

"Now, although she was alarmed, away she ran and I after her to Mr. J...I asked him if he had not landed a cargo of spirits on Thursday night at Swanlake.

'Yes, what of that?'

'Why, lose no time; Mary is gone to Tenby to inform the Custom House officers of it'.

"In less than quarter of an hour, he had eight men, who stole out of Pembroke singly, some by way of Monkton Bridge and over the common, and others through the town, and met at Swanlake, but in an hour he had fifty, all carrying away as fast as possible; the bulk was taken to Sunny

Hill, but a little was stowed away in other safe places, and everything cleared away before Mary returned from Tenby on the Saturday night.

"On Monday morning the Custom House officers came, (they were not very brisk in those days) and went to Mary's house. She guided them to the cellars, where of course they found nothing. Mary, disappointed, said it must be there, as she had seen it all stowed away on Thursday night.

"Mary did not know that I had lived several years as fellow-servant with Mr. J..., a man for whom I had a great regard (especially as he had a family of fourteen children, and it would have ruined him, even had he not been transported), as he had before been convicted of smuggling.

"This was the last smuggling adventure in the neighbourhood, as J...was so alarmed he never ventured another cargo."

Tenby from the North

3

Sea-Dogs and Privateers

A French privateer was once taken by a Tenby pilot Boat. Richard Mason tells the story:

"During the early nineteenth century, a French privateer came into Caldy Roads, when John Tasker, a pilot, not knowing her character (being then out with his boat and men), boarded her; upon going on board, the captain held up his hands crying out "me a prisoner!"

"Tasker secured him before he found out his mistake, and brought his vessel and crew into Tenby harbour, and delivered her up to the Custom House officers. He got a poor return from them, as he was hunted off by the press-gang and, in order to keep his liberty, dared not come to Tenby to claim his share of the prize he had captured. This was the reward for a brave man who served his country".

William Force, or "Daddy Force", was an old sea-dog, who went to sea at the age of eight and could spin a good yarn. He told this tale of his meeting with the Yankee Privateer:

"In November, we had been to Cork in the old 'Gooseberry', the sloop properly called 'The Brothers', with a cargo of oysters. We had disposed of the freight and got abreast of the 'Smalls' on our way home, which we hoped to reach that night. There were a lot of vessels in the Channel, but none on our course eastward, but we soon made out a regular clipper bearing down on us, which fired a gun, then a second gun.

"We let our square-sail go by the run, and lay to until the vessel came up to us, carrying English colours. When she came close, a boat was lowered and manned and pulled alongside. The officer in command jumped on deck.

"Why didn't you heave to when the gun was fired?'
'We didn't think 'twas us you wanted'.
'Where are you from?'
'From Cork'.
'What is your cargo?'
'We're in ballast'.
'What freight had you there?'
'Oysters; and if your honour will come below, I can give you a sample'.

"He came below at once" continues Daddy Force, "and I got out a jar of pickled oysters for him, plenty of 'soft tommy' and new butter. You see they had been all along on biscuit and junk, so that he enjoyed them things. I gave him a drop of whiskey, then says he:

'I think you'd better come on board and see the captain'.

"Well, I didn't like leaving the old 'Gooseberry', but what can a man do when a boat's crew of men-of-war's men are against him? So I asked the officer if he thought the captain would like some such fare, as he'd just had, and as he thought it would do no harm, I got up some jars of oysters, a crock of new butter, and a loaf, got on board the boat and was soon aboard the cruiser. There everything was in place - not an end of rope - guns and small arms done up beautiful.

"I was ordered into the captain's cabin and after asking him if he'd take the present I'd brought for him (which he did quick enough), he got to asking me a lot of questions, all about what men-of-war were in Cork harbour, or had left lately, where they were to cruise and what cruisers were about. I told him all I knew, and when he could get no more out of me he said I was at liberty to go on board my own vessel, but in return for the oysters and butter, I had a fine 'prog' - salt beef, pork, biscuit and rum, as much as I could eat.

"The boat's crew rowed me back to the 'Gooseberry', the vessel at once made sail and stood away to the westward, and as we were getting on our course again, we saw the British ensign hauled down and up went the gridiron flag of Brother Jonathan. I then realised the fellow only wanted information and, as we were the only vessel coming from Ireland, we were the only ones who could give it to him correctly.

"At this time, there was a heavy duty on salt in this country, but none in Ireland, and a lot of smuggling of it used to be carried on. Just as we got abreast of the Milford Islands, we were overhauled by the revenue cutter 'Antelope'. We were boarded by the second officer, who came with us to Tenby, for someone had given them our name as doing a great trade in salt.

"After they'd searched and found nothing, I told him of the encounter with the Yankee, and he was sorry he hadn't heard about it before, as this ship had been plundering, sinking and destroying among the coasters further south. As the Yankee was a fast ship, away on the Western Ocean after our meeting so high up Channel, it would have been impossible to catch up with".

Daddy Force's good seamanship is shown in his voyage to the Isle of Man. When he was in the 'Star' steamer, which traded between Tenby and Bristol, he was asked by Captain Rees if he would take a yacht to the Isle of Man. He was assured by Captain Rees and Mr. Lunell, the Manager of the Bristol Steam Navigation Company, that his berth would be kept open until his return, and that he would be well paid.

On the next voyage to Bristol, he went to look at his yacht and said he would have given all he was worth to be let off his bargain. The yacht was an open boat of about eighteen feet keel, with only "a bit of a cuddy forward into which a man was obliged to creep". But, having undertaken the voyage, he was determined to try it.

Again, he tells the story in his own words:

"We left Bristol about 8 a.m. on a Saturday morning, and having fine weather, reached Milford all safe at midday on Sunday. We were accompanied so far by Captain Kean, who owned the boat. I had orders to get whatever was needed, so I had a canvas deck fitted on amidships. The sailor who came with me from Bristol would go no further, and we shipped a hand known as 'Biscuit Jack'.

"We put to sea about 10 a.m. on a Wednesday morning, with a fair wind, and plenty of it. 'Biscuit Jack' got into the cuddy and was no good to me, being a half crazy kind of fellow.

"The breeze freshened until it blew a perfect gale, but I held my course well for the Irish land. The little boat behaved beautifully although the sea was cross and chopping; my only fear was that a sea might break over her stern, and to avoid that I crossed the mizen seas to be able to steer in pretty good shelter from both wind and sea. About 8 p.m. on Thursday night, I made out the lights on the Calf of Man, and at 10 ran the little craft into Port St. Mary, not sorry to be on dry land, for my rudder had given way and for two hours I had had to steer with an oar. Next morning, we ran for Douglas, where my employer was, and crowds came to see the boat, all wondering how she had lived through such a gale. I stayed at the Isle for five to six weeks, cruising about with the Captain, after which we housed the boat and, besides being paid my wages, I had £10 presented to me and a passage home.

"I afterwards learned that he had won a deal of money on a bet he had made, as a result of the voyage being successfully accomplished. But if ever asked to take a yacht to the Isle of Man again, I shall see before agreeing that she is larger than the one in which that trip was made."

The Pier Head

4

Wrecks

Carmarthen Bay has seen many wrecks, and Tenby also has its memories of disaster. There was, as told later, the loss of the Caldey boat at Christmas time, and an unsolved mystery concerns the disappearance of a local man who went fishing.

Coming back with two other boats and passing between Giltar and St. Margaret's, the three boats were all within sight of each other. Suddenly the middle boat completely vanished from sight and no trace of it, or of any wreckage, was ever found.

Richard Mason gives an elaborate account of "The Wreck of the Brig Richard" at Tenby. The Reverend East was staying on holiday in a house overlooking the South Beach, when he was woken up very early by a storm in the bay. The following is a condensed account of the incident:

There was no sign of an approaching storm on the evening before, 3rd August 1844 but, according to one man who was saved "between one and two in the morning, the sea rose in a moment, the wind gave no warning".

The "Richard", a brig of Sunderland of about 250 tons burden, lay at anchor upon a hard sand-bank far out from the shore. She lay there for nearly two hours, then the flowing tide lifted her off, but she had also lost her rudder. Her crew of seven found that she had also sprung a formidable leak, which they could not counteract by pumping. They continued to make every attempt to save the ship, spreading all the canvas they could, and trying to make for Tenby harbour. During these three hours, they sent out all the distress signals, but the tempest raged and, when dawn came, they were still in difficulties.

The Reverend East discovered the brig at about four o'clock and realised her danger. The fury of the storm woke him, and he saw the vessel coming straight before the wind to the shore below the house. She seemed to be sinking, then she struck so violently that the captain and mate were thrown down the companion stairs, the cabin being full of water. The mate drowned and the captain was seriously injured.

The sea was so rough that the men could not leap overboard to swim to shore, and in great distress they threw everything they could over the side. A boat was lowered and one bold seaman leapt into it, but this boat was swamped in heavy seas and he was drowned. The ship rolled on, mountainous waves rushed over her deck, the masts and timbers cracked and broke. No lifeboat then existed upon the shore. The survivors, one the bleeding captain, took to the rigging, but soon the mainmast crashed over and they were thought to have drowned or been crushed by the falling timbers.

"The vessel drove on furiously to the base of the cliffs" says the Reverend East, "when it was seen that the five men were still alive almost within reach. Three cowered down by the windlass, two were on the bowsprit. These two were William Cook, captain and master, and Robert Clasper, a seaman. No help had reached the ship by 7 a.m., but then a brass mortar (with Captain Manby's apparatus, an impressive contrivance for throwing an iron ball with grappling hooks), and a rope attached to it, was brought into operation from a projecting part of the cliffs."

At last, a rope was successfully thrown to the ship. Robert Clasper fastened its loop around him and plunged into the sea. But the rope had become entangled in the wreck and he was drowned. He was twenty-eight and left a widow and a child. William Cook, the captain, fell into the sea and was also drowned; this was on the day his wife gave birth to their fourth child.

The captain's brother, who was injured, was drawn up the rocks, one young apprentice was drowned and a lad of sixteen was eventually saved when yet another ball was fired from the cannon's mouth on the cliff, carrying a rope. He fastened the noose round his waist, plunged into the sea and was rescued.

"After eighteen hours of struggle in the storm, three men were saved from the wreck of the Brig Richard".

At the turn of the century, a French barque of Nantes, was on her voyage home from the west coast of Africa, carrying a cargo of oil nuts. The captain and mate were taken ill, so the ship lost her bearings and found herself in Carmarthen Bay.

Some of the local seamen went out and arranged to bring the ship into the Harbour. As the ship was lightly built and therefore only suitable for anchorage in deep water, one of the older seamen said that it would not be possible for her to leave the Harbour again.

In spite of this, after a message had been sent to Nantes, the barque was brought in to await orders. When she was high and dry at the first ebb tide, her seams began to open and she became a wreck, breaking up with every subsequent tide. Local carters took away large quantities of the oil-nuts for pay, in an attempt to save the cargo, and stored them, but they were valueless locally. After three weeks, the ship was empty and broken up, so everything that could be salvaged from it was taken away and sold for any money that could be raised.

At last, the owner's agent arrived in Tenby, and took a very poor view of the whole disreputable business, as it was said that some of the Breton sailors had had to fight off the local people with knives.

Foundation of South Wall

5

The Tenby Lifeboat

The old Lifeboat House used to stand at the bottom of the slope to the Castle Beach, and the boat was launched by hand. When it could not be launched from the Castle Beach it was pulled along by ropes to be launched from the South Beach instead. Each launch was attended by a tally-woman who gave a disc or tally to all those people who had helped at a launching, and this tally would then be exchanged for money.

Gosse (1810 - 1888), who was working on the marine life of the Tenby beaches, gives the following description:

"Looking out just now I saw a great crowd on the quay, and groups of people eagerly running through the street to join them. I seized my hat and went down too, a boatman informing me that they were going to have some lifeboat practice.

When I got to the quay, I saw a great awkward-looking craft, painted light blue, very much curved in her shear, and rising to a high peak at each end. Seven or eight young fellows were putting on jackets made of parallel strips of cork bound together. Presently, three or four of them jump overboard and being sufficiently buoyant in their cork armour play rude frolics in the water. The others prepare to turn the lifeboat over.

"For this purpose they brought a lighter alongside her and, having first girded her with two bands of rope, made fast a chair to these and hooked it on to the quay-crane.

'Now then, all right?'

'Wind away!''

The fellows who suffer the experiment... have stow'd themselves away in the bottom of the boat, beneath the thwarts, which they grasp with nervous energy in their arms. The windlass turns and turns, creaking musically, the chain goes up and up, dragging one side of the boat with it. Presently over she heels, the lads grasping the thwarts and looking very blue, as she turns her somersault. The crowds give a huge hurrah, as up she comes, righting herself in a moment; the men splash and splutter, dash away the water from their hairy faces, and grin at the cheering spectators ashore.

"I find it is a new boat, as yet untried, made on a new principle by Beecher of North Yarmouth. The principle was described to me as consisting of air-boxes in her sides, so that it is impossible she should ever fill, the water not being able to rise in her beyond a certain bearing. Her curved form prevents her lying capsized as was shown in the experiment, while it gives great facilities in turning, a single stroke of the steering oars moving the boat as on a centre.

"I thought the exhibition one of the most interesting things I had seen here...."

"The Tenby Souvenir", a Table-Book in Prose and Verse, written by Mrs. F.P. Gwynne was illustrated by Charles Allen and published by Richard Mason in 1863. It tells of the wreck of the "Nuevo Torcuvato" from which the Tenby Lifeboat saved all the men on board in the late 1850's. It describes the Lifeboat as "built on the self-righting plan, 28' long by 7'6" wide, and says that it "has given assistance to eight wrecked vessels and saved the crew of four, viz. the Agenora of Bideford, Alexandre of Nantes, Nuevo Torcuvato of Valencia and Breeze of Milford.

The table book says:

"Mr. Parrot, Coast Guard Officer, lives in the Watch House on the Castle Hill; receives donations for the society and is always ready, with the crew of sturdy men, to put off in the wildest weather in the lifeboat, and to assist equally with his crew on shore, when rockets are required to convey ropes from cliffs to the crews of vessels stranded among the rocks. By this means the crews are enabled to draw an apparatus across the rope from the cliff, in which, one by one, they are drawn safely from the mast to the land."

When the brig "Policy", of Sunderland, was wrecked beneath the steep cliff at Trevane, on the North Sands, the crew were desperate as the lifeboat could not get near to the wreck. The sea smashed their oars and they had to return to the Harbour.

After a wild night, the captain with a broken arm, was drawn up the cliff, completely disabled, and the crew were safely brought off the wreck also and taken into Tenby.

"Brave men were ever ready to assist the unfortunate, before life-boats had been seen here. The Tenby sailors never saw a ship in distress, without trying to reach it - always eager and ready to brave the storm... As regards braving danger, at a time of shipwreck - in this respect Tenby men may well challenge comparison with any men in the world."

Among the daring members of the old crews was Benny Nash, a resolute bold man with fierce appearance, stout-built and powerful. He used very strong language and was a good fighter. "As an angel of life he appeared to many a half-drowned seaman".

In one terrific storm, the men were turned back from attempting to save two ships in distress, and being exhausted, they came to Castle Hill to see the disaster. One vessel was then on the shore. Nash turned doggedly round and said:

"I ain't going to stay here and see them men drown."
And then added:
"I'm going, who's coming along wi' me?"

All the men were instantly in their places and set out again. They were often lost to view on the foaming sea, but they succeeded in saving all the crew.

Other members of the rescue crews were Thomas Hall, George Watkins, William John, and John Ray who was a native of New Providence, the Bahamas, and a clever diver and swimmer. His extreme bravery was shown on one occasion when the sloop William, of Fishguard, was driven on the cliffs near Waterwynch:

"The boats got as close to the wreck as safety would permit, and floated ropes to the vessel, signing to the crew to fasten them round their waists, then leaping clear of the wreck, to be quickly drawn to the boat, whose crew held the end of the ropes. Thus many lives had often been saved, but the men on board were stupefied by exposure and terror.

"An intelligent little boy on the wreck alone seemed to understand how to act; he tied a rope round his waist. At this time the apparatus of Captain Manby had succeeded in firing ropes from the cliff over the vessel, this being an easier way of escaping. The little boy first tied ropes round the two men; and after they had been each drawn ashore in safety, his own turn came.

"Forgetting first to undo the rope he had fastened round himself from the boat, the poor boy adjusted the other shore-line, and leaped off, but the loose rope was twined by the breakers round the wreck, and thus pulled him down to the deck."

The people on shore and the crew tried to release the boy, but John Ray, seeing the cause of the trouble, leaped into the sea and soon stood on the wreck himself. He unfortunately found he had lost his knife. They tried to undo the knotted rope until the young half-drowned boy said: "It's no use trying to save me; if you don't go away, you will be drowned too - never mind me, do save yourself".

Ray stayed with the boy, who died in his arms, then he somehow managed to reach his own boat, which had been kept afloat in the rough sea, endangering the crew.

One fine day, Benny Nash, his two sons, and Louis Bowen went out to draw their lobster pots near the Old Castle Head. It was assumed that the four men had all gone on to one side of their boat in a heavy swell, for the boat capsized and the four men were drowned.

"The body of Nash was never found: of his sons, one was picked up, and brought home to be buried; the other was washed on shore at. Ferryside, and rests there. Bowen was found among the caverns at Lydstep."

Between 1855 and the present day, there have been five Lifeboats in service, the "Florence" (1855 - 1885), the "Anne Collins" (1886 - 1901), the "William and Mary Devey" (1902 - 1923), the "John R. Webb" (1923 - 1955), and the "Henry Comber Brown" (1955 -), which have saved 417 lives and 35 vessels.

The R.N.L.I's Silver and Bronze Medals have been awarded to members of the Tenby Lifeboat crew, and there is a strong family tradition of service in the town.

19th. century Tenby Lifeboat

6

Temperament and Way of Life

The temperament of Pembrokeshire people was noted by Edward Laws, who commented on their "good humour and cheerfulness, charm of manner and a peculiarly pleasant voice. They are", he said, "kindly folk, gentle to women and children, and merciful of animals. A love of making things pleasant mitigates against truth. It is hopeless to expect an exact statement. Disagreeable angles are rounded off."

Their clannishness was strong, and he said: "Love children abound and a girl who has 'tripped' is not considered to have erred very grievously". They were "good horsemen and bold soldiers, unlike the Welshmen", they had Norse characteristics, and were "heavy drinkers but not quarrelsome, extremely hospitable, thrifty, but lack enterprise and save rather than make money. Slovenly in their houses, persons and work, curiously unaesthetic, but passionately fond of music, god-fearing and law-abiding."

He summed up by stating that "despite certain transparent naughtinesses" they were "most lovable".

The nickname of "Leekie Porridge", given to one of Tenby's local characters, is also explained by Edward Laws. Cock-a-leekie porridge was broth made of fowl and leeks. This was eaten at the Cymmorth, which was "an assembly of friends to help a neighbour in haymaking, corn harvest, ploughing, carrying limestone" etc. The host found the materials for this leekie porridge, which was eaten by the guests, but each one provided his own leek and "as it was the custom to carry it in their hats, the leek became the national emblem of Wales". There are, however, many other explanations.

In the past, food used to be plentiful but rough, and mostly bacon. Washporo, which was oatmeal containing the bran, boiled into gruel then fermented and boiled again, before being made into an opaque jelly eaten cold with milk, was a favourite Pembrokeshire dish. George Owen thought the Welsh, who lived on mainly milk, butter and cheese, better-looking than the "Englishry", who fed on so much meat. Later, Edward Laws said that the English inhabitants of Pembrokeshire ate heavily taking seven meals a day, five usually, "the poorest husbandmen feeding daily on beef, mutton, pig, goose, lamb, veal or kid".

Well-to-do farmers made strong ale, which was charged with malt to saturation point. Cellared for many years, it became clear-amber coloured, and was then as strong as brandy. The leavings were made into 'small beer'.

A local Tenby resident told the author that, in about 1493 - 1505, a Portuguese cargo ship was passing by. A few oranges, the crew's ration, were thrown into the sea off Tenby, and this was the first time that oranges had been seen in this country.

Cottages were once built of clom, which was clay mixed with chopped straw, and had one room, or occasionally two, in which a culm fire burned summer and winter. Culm was anthracite dust mixed with clay, and this was trodden until it blended, and then stacked. Fires did not blaze but, when once lighted, never went out. Each night, a thick coat of the clayey compound was laid like a plaster on the fire. By morning, the layer was hard and hot and was used as a cooking surface. The fire was then stoked down and the top covered with balls of culm formed by hand, which lasted all day and could bear the weight of a saucepan or kettle. These fires, used in Tenby kitchens, kept down the cost of living. A small export trade of coal from Saundersfoot kept the harbour busy in the 1860's, but by 1919 only one pit remained workable.

In the past, cottages were lighted by tiny windows, which were not meant to open, sometimes consisting of only a single pane. The floor was of beaten clay and the roof of unceilinged thatch. The pig, which had its own house, wandered everywhere and was fed on much the same food as the family. An iron pot, from which everyone once used to eat, contained broken barley bread, garden vegetables, and water thickened with meal. Caldey and St. David's were renowned for their barley and oats, and Castlemartin produced the best wheat, most of which was consumed in the county. By the beginning of the nineteenth century, breeding black Castlemartin cattle was the staple industry of the area.

The following item appears in the Order Book at Tenby, for March 30th 1784:

'Tis observed by the Mayor and Council that great numbers of pigs are suffered to go about the streets of this Borough, which is become an insufferable nuisance to the inhabitants thereof; 'tis therefore thought necessary to appoint Thomas Harris and Abraham Richard, two constables to impound all pigs that shall be found going about the streets and environs of this Borough in the common pound . . ."

In old Pembrokeshire lanes, it was said that pigs possessed by the Devil could be seen in lonely haunted places. Owing to comman rights, pigs were allowed to graze freely on village greens and around houses, for example at Begelly and Gumfreston, and as above at Tenby.

For clothing, brown homespun used to be worn, which kept out cold and rain. The women wore a short petticoat and jacket, a close cap with long lappets and a straw or felt hat, the wife usually, and children always, went barefoot. On high days only, the Welsh hat was produced. Farmers, wives and daughters rode to market on horseback, with huge baskets of butter and eggs slung by their sides. They wore the tall churn-shaped Welsh hat, under which a white handkerchief was bound round their heads. "They knitted on pins continually indoors and out, noon and night". This was said by Edward Laws in his "Gentleman's Tour", printed in 1775. He also said:

"The dress of Pembroke women differs from the rest of Wales. Even in the midst of summer, they wear a heavy cloth gown, and instead of a cap a large handkerchief wrapt over their heads and tied under their chins. This custom is certainly peculiar to Pembrokeshire."

A friend of Edward Laws, who was educated at Tenby Parochial Schools, said that in 1847 Mr. Dashwood "grieving that the bare feet of children should rest all day on the cold stones, had the building floored at his own expense." In the year 1888, it was impossible to find a barefooted child in the town of Tenby.

Allen's "Guide to Tenby" provides a more detailed account of the Pembrokeshire national costume:

"This costume consisted of a high-crowned black beaver hat set on the extreme top of the head; a white stiffly starched cap under it, and the brown cloth tight jacket, with short plain sleeves. The jacket is well calculated to show the figure to advantage. It is a most becoming dress, the light neckerchief under it and bright coloured cotton sleeves attached to the short cloth ones, with the addition, in general, of bright blue or garnet-coloured glass buttons at the back and sleeves of the jacket, the short petticoat of brown cloth, and black and white apron, black stockings and shoes." In the same Guide, the Llangwm oyster women are described. They used to be seen in the streets of Tenby, with their creels or panniers slung behind them, with straps of leather fastening them over their shoulders.

"They row their boats in Milford Haven waters, dredging for oysters, and afterwards walk thence to Tenby to dispose of the oysters to the visitors."

"Betty Palmer" was faithfully represented in photographic groups of these oyster women.

Oyster shells, which were the refuse of the pickling industry, used to form a mound below the Whitesand Gate, and remained there until the 1930's.

The population of Tenby grew rapidly in the mid-nineteenth century, as can be seen in the following table:

Census of Population

1801	-	844
1821	-	1,400
1831	-	1,942
1851	-	3,200
1978	-	4,985

Hunting was widely practised, and a contributor to the Cambrian Register in 1795 stated that it was very much in fashion, especially in the Fishguard and Haverfordwest areas. But an even earlier date is given to an old hunting song, which was given to Edward Laws by Mr. Wade of Tenby, which a Mr. Llewellyn of Tarr had given him in turn. Only two verses remain:

"On Saturday last, about four in the morn,
I rode by the cry and the sound of the horn;
The stars being bright, the morning seemed fair,
So I slipped on my boots and mounted my mare.
    Right, tol de rol, dol" &c.

"I rode by the cry and the sound of the horn
Till I came to the Hill of Gumfreston Ground;
There I met with Frank Meyrick, and hunters the score,
All right jolly fellows, I'd met them before.
    Right, tol de rol, dol" &c.

About 1750, a daring gang of mounted freebooters spread terror through the county. One farmer was set upon by three of them, but he fought them off with his heavily loaded hunting whip!

In his "Customs of Little England in the 12th Century", Gerald de Barri describes the people as very musical, playing three instruments, the harp, flute or pipe and an instrument resembling the violin, the crwth - with the upper part of the bridge flat, so that all the strings are sounded at once. He adds that they were very fond of vocal music, especially part singing.

According to the Treasure of Folklore No. 26 "Lore and Legend of Pembrokeshire edited by S. Jackson Coleman, tune applied firstly to the words, and not the music, in local dialect. There were many "tunes of one breath", and the verses which began briefly and could be sung by those not expert in breath control, became increasingly difficult as they went on, becoming longer and longer. Eventually it was almost impossible to complete the last verse of the song.

At night, the whole household lay down together to sleep, in their usual clothing for greater warmth, on a common bed of rushes strewn on the floor near to the slow-burning culm fire. In Gerald's time, this led to his accusations of promiscuity. He said that couples always cohabited before marriage, to test the disposition and fecundity of their intended partner, and parents hired out their daughters for a given price, with a stipulated fine in case connection was relinquished. He accused the Welsh of incest, or marrying within the prohibited degrees.

Ancient Cottage near Market

7

Courting, a Welsh Bidding, the Ceffyl Prên

the Welsh custom of Bundling, or courting abed, is well-known, and took place especially in rural areas. When labourers worked extremely long hours, their only free time was late at night. Wirt Sikes, in his "British Goblins" (1880), comments on this tradition, which was severely condemned by the Church, but also says:
"Courtship was anciently guarded by the sternest laws, so that any other issue to courtship than marriage was practically impossible. A girl who forgot her duty to herself and family was thrown over a precipice, and the young man also destroyed." The Reverend G. Huntington in his book "Random Reflections", when writing about the Reverend G. Smith of Gumfreston, tells the following tale:
"The lax notions of Welsh people on courtship and matrimony are only too well known, the custom of 'bundling' and of courting at unseemly hours has not yet died out. A stalwart youth thought he would try it on at Gumfreston Rectory. Smith caught him in the kitchen when the family were thought to be at rest, so he took him by the shoulders and pushed him into a cupboard where he locked him up and kept him 'in durance vile' until the morning.
"The next Sunday, the banns were published and the sermon was on what would now be called 'social morality'.
Lovespoons were intricately carved by young men, and there are some

survivals of intricately embroidered valentines. In the long dark winter evenings, divination was practised.

At Tenby, on All-Hallow's-eve, girls would go alone to cross-roads at midnight, and having raised a little of the ground, would sow some hemp-seed and then sing:

"Hemp seed I sow
Hemp seed I'll mow
Whoe'er my true love is to be
Come rake this hemp seed after me."

It was said that the shape of the person looked for came and raked the hemp seed, while some of the sowers were frightened by actually feeling the rake touch their legs. This custom also took place in England and Scotland, and was practised on Midsummer Eve at midnight. At both these times of the year, it was believed that the real and the unseen worlds overlapped.

A second method of divination was to lay a table in the hall or kitchen with meat and drink, leaving a lighted candle. A wet article of woman's clothing was hung over a chair before the fire. The girl would then hide, probably in a cupboard, waiting patiently to see whether anyone would come and turn the article. If they appeared and did this, the girl expected to be a bride in the same year, but sometimes the apparition of a coffin was seen instead of a person.

There was a third method, which was introduced into Pembrokeshire by the Flemings. Nine holes were bored in the blade bone of a shoulder of mutton, then the bone was put under the pillow before going to sleep. Shoes were placed at the foot of the bed in the shape of a letter T, while these words were recited:

"I put my shoes in the shape of a T,
Hoping my true love for to see,
Not in apparel or array,
But in his clothes he wears every day".

In Pembrokeshire, a tea leaf which floated on a cup of tea was said to mean that a young man or woman would have a new sweetheart. Several leaves meant a choice, and the length of the leaf denoted his or her height. The leaf was picked out and, when placed on the back of the hand, a transfer to the other hand was attempted. If this was successful the first time, it meant the sweetheart's arrival within a week; if at the second time, within a fortnight, and so on.

If a girl was anxious to know whom she would marry, she could steal a turnip from a neighbour's field. After washing this in salted water, it had to be peeled carefully in one continuous strip, beginning at the top of the turnip and finishing at the bottom. If it was broken, or cracked, the spell would not work. The clean turnip was hung up behind the kitchen door and the peel buried in the garden. The first person of the opposite sex who came into the kitchen, would have the same name as the girl's future husband.

When a wedding had been decided upon, a Bidding took place. Richard Mason describes this custom in "Tales and Traditions of Tenby". It was still in use in the mid-nineteenth century among the small farmers and respectable labourers in Pembrokeshire and the adjoining counties.

"When two young people were about to marry, their parents, or nearest relatives, procured the services of a 'lavier' (levyer or collector), who set out to carry an invitation and welcome to the wedding dinner, giving a humorous account of the prepared feast. The guests were chosen in this way: the parents and the engaged couple took account of the different weddings they had attended, and looked upon the presents given as debts owing to them, which would now be repaid. A list of those by whom 'gifts' were returnable was given to the 'levyer' who distributed printed circulars to the intended guests, or told them of the date and time of the wedding."

"The invitation would read as follows:

'We are encouraged by our friends to make a Bidding on Tuesday the 23rd instant, at ...., where your most agreeable company will be humbly solicited by your humble servants,

       Thomas ....
       Mary ....

'NB. The young woman's father and mother, Thomas and Sarah ......, and her brothers and sister, Benjamin, John, Evan, Maurice and Sarah, desire that all gifts of the above nature will be returned to the young woman on that day; and whatever donation you may be pleased to bestow on them will be warmly acknowledged, and cheerfully repaid, whenever called for on a similar occasion.'

"All the company assemble on the day of the marriage and, after the ceremony, partake of the feast. When this is finished, the 'bidding' commences, each guest making a point of returning the value of the gifts they had received at their own 'bidding'.

"In some cases, donations consisted of bread, butter, cheese etc; in others articles of farming stock, or household furniture; so that if the parents and relatives, and the young couple, had been liberal themselves at biddings the returns were proportionally great.

"On the 'nos blaen', or night preceding the wedding, friends of the bride and bridegroom assembled at the house where the wedding was to be held and beer and cakes were sold and consumed then, and on the wedding day, as a source of gain for the couple."

Three copies of Welsh Bidding letters are preserved in Tenby Museum library.

In some parts of the county, bride, bridegroom and friends went mounted to Church. When the service was completed, the newly-married couple galloped home as fast as they could, pursued by their friends. If the bride was caught, friends were entitled to a kiss and the bridegroom had to ransom his new wife with unlimited supplies of "Cwrw dda" (good beer).

This custom is a relic of the ancient tribal laws which forbade a man to choose a wife from his own tribe. If his own tribe were at war with neighbouring factions, he had to steal his bride. Marriage by capture was later commemorated by a race for a kiss and a cup of beer.

The savage custom of lynch law also prevailed. When there was domestic strife, and a woman "dictated to her husband, with many blows", the neighbours brought round the "Ceffyl prên", or wooden horse". An effigy in the likeness of the offender was seated on a chair and placed on a ladder. This was carried on men's shoulders, with a crowd preceding and following the "Ceffyl prên" in procession, screaming and beating on tin saucepans. They stopped at times and the spokesman then described the offence:

"Ran-dan-dan.
Betty Morris has beat her man"
"What was it with?"
"'Twas not with a rake, nor yet with a reel,
But 'twas with a poker, that made him feel".

When a man or woman broke their marriage vows, the mob, not content with an effigy, seized and fastened them back to back, mounting them on the wooden horse, and paraded them about, proclaiming their shame. They pelted them with rotten eggs and other missiles. After some time, they were taken down and followed with hoots and jeers to their house, where they were left "to cope with the reproaches of their injured partners".

8

Birth and Death

There used to be a charming old custom in Pembrokeshire of giving a small frock to the mother at the birth of her first-born child. Relations and friends used to compete with eath other to bring the prettiest and most useful frock, and sometimes about fifty were presented in this way. A list of the donors was carefully kept, and the garments were placed on display until the child had been "tucked" or taken out of long clothes.

Mischievous fairies were especially active after the birth of a child, and could even carry away the mother before she had been "churched" at a special ceremony after the birth. To avoid this and to deceive the spirits, her husband's clothes were spread over her. There was also fear that a changeling or fairy child might be substituted, and so a piece of iron, a metal taboo to fairies, was stitched into the baby's clothes and salt sprinkled into the cradle.

Babies' nails were never cut but were bitten off by the mother. In a year's time, the nails would have regrown their whole length and an edged tool could then be used. It was thought that an infant whose nails were cut off would develop into a thief.

A more gruesome custom was to christen an infant over the corpse of its mother, if she died in childbirth, and this was a primitive form of baptism called "Bedydd-arch".

Children would not do certain things, for fear of becoming a bird, cat or dog in a future life, a relic of retributive reincarnation.

Hair was never thrown away or destroyed, but buried in a "claddgwallt", usually in a hedge or garden wall, by the owner of the hair. It must never be thrown into a stream or calamities would take place. This is told in "Glossary of the Demetian Dialect" by Meredith Morris, p.69 and quoted by S. Jackson Coleman.

Death customs were strange and elaborate and many portents were observed. Catherine Wyatt of Tenby saw two lights hovering over her body, and these were considered an omen of death. Shortly afterwards, she gave birth to still-born twins.

It was a trial of courage to stand at the Church door on All-Hallows'-eve, listening in silence. As soon as the last stroke of midnight had sounded, you might expect to hear the names of each person who would die in the parish within the following year.

Many signs were awaited with dread: the tolaeth, a speaking voice just before the time of death; the cyhyraeth, a groaning spirit; the aderyn y corph, a chirping bird at the door or window; also the canwyll corph or corpse candle, a small pale blue or white flame, varying with age and sex of the person concerned, which hovered over the body. There were also the cŵn annwn, the hounds of hell, who hunted the souls of the dead, the gwrach y rhibyn, an ugly female banshee, as well as spots, spirits, a headless horse and carriage, the Welsh parallel to the Irish death-coach.

Edward Laws describes a local fetch or phantom funeral:

"A man in the employment of the Vicar of Penally one morning assured his master that, on the previous evening, he had met a large funeral procession near Holloway Farm, and named several neighbours among the mourners. The vicar laughed at him.

"But," said the man, "the most curious thing was that they carried the coffin over a bank."

"Then surely", answered his master, "you can show me the place, for so large a party could not have passed over a bank without trampling it down."

The man pointed out a place in the narrow lane near Holloway Farm, assuring his master that, at that particular point, the funeral party left the road and passed over a bank into a field. There were no signs of such a passage.

Shortly afterwards, Mr. Williams, the tenant of Holloway, died and, as a snowdrift blocked up this lane, his coffin was carried over the bank at the spot pointed out on its way to the graveyard of Penally.

A phantom funeral funeral was also seen at Tenby. A ghostly procession passed by, in which each of the participants was recognised by the surprised onlooker. The person seen as the corpse was always expected to die shortly after the procession took place.

The Editor of "Tales and Traditions of Tenby", Richard Mason, tells this anecdote of two ladies of his family, who were returning home one winter's evening from a market town not a dozen miles from Tenby:

"Being rather late, several members of the family rushed to the doors to receive them, while others went to the windows with lights. The next day, the gardener was gravely told by one of the villagers that a death was going to occur in the family, for he had seen the corpse lights at the doors and windows, and also had watched the hearse draw up to the door, stay long enough to take up a corpse, and then drive off towards the churchyard, when it disappeared.

"The spectator and prophet was much disappointed when the servant confirmed that the carriage had conveyed the ladies home, only stopped to set them down, and then driven back by the road above the churchyard, where it could not be seen on account of the trees that overhung the road!"

Edward Laws quotes what, to him, was a recent case of a phantom funeral, taking place in the mid 1880's, but he gives no names or location for it:

"A Nonconformist minister invited a neighbouring preacher to pay him a visit, and took a bedroom for his guest over a little shop. The friend, an elderly man in bad health, retired to bed early. Shortly afterwards, the shopkeeper, while making up his books, was terrified to see two carpenters he knew come down the stairs from the guest room carrying a coffin, which they took out of the house without a word.

"The shopkeeper, nearly frightened out of his wits, told the strange minister what he had seen, when the latter came down in the morning. While they were still discussing this matter, the other minister came in, and with a cry, threw up his arms and staggered back falling down in a fit of apoplexy. They carried him upstairs and laid him down on his friend's bed where, shortly afterwards, he died. The carpenters were then set for, who put the corpse in a shell and carried it down the stairs to the dead man's own house."

At wake and funeral ceremonies, strong ale known as "termont" was brewed, and the following account was sent to a Pembrokeshire newspaper by a contributor many years ago:

"The ale was served by two men on the funeral day - one carrying the hot ale and the other the cold ale. The people formed a semi-circle and those who carried the ale commenced helping them at one end following around".

It was said that many of the company changed places, so as to receive many helpings! It was:

"nothing extraordinary, therefore, to see a number of drunken men at a funeral, before starting from the house to the graveyard. While the men were carrying round the termont outside the house, two women, with white towels pinned on their left arm, would at the same time be engaged in distributing white and red wine to the special guests who were assembled inside."

It was regular practice to watch the dead and, when a person died, candles were immediately brought in by the neighbours and friends. A member of the family sat up with the corpse and, the night before the funeral, immense numbers went to the house, to the room where the corpse was laid out. This was called the "Wylnos" or "Watch-night".

An account of an old-time wake is given in the antiquaries' column of the "Pembroke County Guardian", dated 2nd May 1896:

"Although this old custom of watching and illuminating the chamber of the dead is still practised, it has lost all its most peculiar features, namely, the drawing up of the corpse through the chimney of the house where the death had occurred before it was conveyed to its last resting-place. "The process of this extraordinary and mysterious custom was as follows:

"A certain number of persons would be engaged to remove the corpse from its coffin to a convenient place near the fire, where the pinioning of the dead would be performed. This was effected by tying a rope to the upper part of the body, the other end being afterwards passed up the chimney by means of a long stick or pitchfork. Then a sufficient number of men, possible according to the weight of the corpse, would be sent to the top of the chimney on the outside of the roof, which they reached by the help of a ladder, for the purpose of hauling up the corpse. These, having first fixed themselves as securely as the perilous nature of the situation would allow, took hold of the rope and signalled to the party inside by crying 'Hir wen gwd!' (words probably referring to the long white shroud with which the body was wrapt) and the party inside answered 'Whave'n barod!' (words equivalent to 'We are ready!'), and slowly but surely up the chimney went the corpse. When it had been brought to the top, it was carefully lowered again, and eventually replaced in its coffin."

Everyone who wished to show respect to the dead person attended the funeral, and a short religious service was often performed at the house before the funeral procession, which moved to the burial ground singing verses of psalms or hymns, with a small knot of singers acting as a leading choir.

The same road, known as the "Funeral" or "Church" road was always followed. If it should lead through a field of corn, this would make no difference, and messengers went ahead to warn owners of fields on the previous day to clear a path. A woman walked before the procession with a basket of evergreens, including bay and box sprigs, dropping them on the road at intervals, but keeping a few sprays to drop on to the coffin in the grave.

If ground was consecrated, this must always lie fallow, and if the site of an old burial ground came into the corner of a fruitful field, this portion was always left untouched.

When the east wind blew on Christmas Eve, this was propitious. The wind was called "gwynt traed i meirw" (the wind blowing over the feet of the corpses), because it blew towards the foot of the graves in the churchyard. This originated in the custom of burying the dead in churchyards with their feet, and their faces, turned to the east.

The Conduit

9

Ghosts, the "Little Fair Folk", Charmers and Witches

There are many stories of the supernatural in the Tenby area, but these tales lingered on mainly in the villages, where young girls and boys, returning home from fairs, wakes or wedding parties, were once frightened by the "Nameless One" with his clanking chains, and by roaming pigs said to be possessed by the Devil.

They also dreaded finding a fairy circle, as then it was vital to look away and to creep past so as not to disturb the "Dynon Bach Teg", the "Little Fair Folk", as they were known in Pembrokeshire, at their mystic revels. If they saw you, they would insist on you joining in, and you would either be unable to stop dancing until you fell exhausted, or you might be spirited away to a land where time was not the same as you knew on earth. Sometimes you would return home from this place, after having broken a taboo and been released from their enchanted land, to find that you had been away for many generations and were a stranger in your own house. If you got lost at night you were said in the English-speaking parts of Pembrokeshire, to be "pisky-led". The "Little Fair Folk" are usually known in Wales as the Tylwyth Teg, the "Fair Tribe".

In the following story, the time barrier had the opposite effect to that mentioned above. This version was told by Hartland in his book on the "Science of Fairy Tales" (pp.225-6) and there are many varying accounts of this experience in Welsh folklore:

A young man, who joined a fairy dance, found himself in a palace glittering with gold and pearls. He stayed there for many years, until one day out of curiosity, he broke his promise not to drink from a certain well, where golden and coloured fishes swam. As soon as he plunged his hand into the water, everything vanished away and a shriek rang out through the garden. He found himself on the hillside with his father's flocks around him. What had seemed years had, in fact, only been the few minutes during which he had been spell-bound, and he had never left the sheep at all.

Many people claimed to have seen fairies shopping in town markets in Wales. Wirt Sikes, who was United States Consul for Wales, published his "British Goblins" (1880), and describes the faries shopping in Milford Haven and Laugharne markets:

"They made their purchases without speaking, laid down their money and departed, always leaving the exact sum required, which they seemed to know, without asking the price of anything. Sometimes they were invisible, but they were often seen by sharp-eyed persons. There was always one special butcher at Milford Haven upon whom the fairies bestowed their patronage, instead of distributing their favours indiscriminately.

"The Milford Haven folk could see the green fairy islands distinctly, lying out a short distance from land, and the general belief was they they were densely peopled with fairies. It was also said that the latter went to and fro between the islands and the shore through a subterranean gallery under the bottom of the sea."

Charles Squire, in "Celtic Myth and Legend", says that the Green Meadows of Enchantment", said to be seen occasionally off the Pembrokeshire coast, "are still an article of faith among Pembrokeshire and Carmarthenshire sailors, not without reason".

John Rhys in "The Arthurian Legend" (1891) mentions that men had landed on these islands. According to Wirt Sikes, they were supposed to float a few feet beneath the surface of the sea and appear and disappear.

Various surprising beliefs about the origin of the "Little Fair Folk", have been put forward. The "Treasury of Folklore" notes the following theories: they were thought to be the spirits of anvient druids, descendants of conquered aborigines, or the descendants of a woman cursed by her own sister, who was possessed by a devil, exorcised by Christ!

The various elements of folk belief on this subject are classified by W. J. Gruffydd in "Folklore and Myth in the Mabinogion" (University of Wales Press).

Everywhere there were thought to be spirits and demons who could be summoned up inadvertently, especially by whistling, and it is still considered unlucky to whistle in Welsh mines or at sea. Green, a colour associated with various diminutive beings such as fairies, is still an unpopular colour in Welsh rural areas.

At times, ghost laying needed to be performed. A delegation once came from St. Florence to Dr. Humphreys, then Rector of Tenby, to ask him to lay a ghost which haunted the parish. This tale is told by the Reverend G. Hungtindon, Rector of Tenby, in his "Random Reflections" published in 1896. He asked why they had come to see him, when they had a parson of their own. They explained that only an Oxford scholar could lay a ghost!

"I am afraid", said the Rector, who did not wish to give offence, but wanted to be let off the ordeal, "you have come to the wrong man; for you see, I am a Cambridge man!"

Thomas Athroe served as Mayor of Tenby in the eighteenth century. With his son he quarrelled with George Marchant, during the November fair at Wiston over some cattle, which they said had been bought out of their hands. The Athroes murdered George Marchant under the small bridge by Holloway Water, and the Mayor's ghost used to haunt this bridge.

The Phantom Carriage of Stackpole Court was said to travel from Tenby to Sampson Cross Roads, near Stackpole. The party consisted of two horses, a coachman and a lady, who were all headless! The lady was popularly styled "Lady Mathias". The appearance of the carriage was said to foretell some momentous happening, often a death, in the family of the owners of the Court, which is now a ruin.

It is also said in the "Treasury of Folklore" that an apparition seen near Pembroke, consisting of a headless spectre, coachman and team of horses, all headless, was that of Mrs. Jean Mansel, who was buried in St. Petroc's Church.

On the site of the old Priory in Frog Street, Tenby, a resident told the author that a white monk had been seen recently in one of the present houses.

Gray's "Guide to Tenby" says that a White Lady used to appear infrequently in Tenby to indicate the spot where hidden treasure was buried.

An extraordinary and inexplicable story appeared in "The Daily Express" for 28th May 1934, concerning the earth-bound spirit of a sixth-century nun. In this story, the vicar of Monkton, the Reverend Tudor Evans, told this newspaper's correspondent that he had lived with his family in the Old Hall for some time. He believed that this had once been a Priory, under which was a large groined crypt, and that some of the rooms there had been cells. Every morning at four o'clock, the vicar continued, he heard a heavy knocking on his bedroom door, but this was never traced to any proper cause. His dog refused to go into one of the rooms. One day, his daughter saw a glow in this same room and what appeared to be a figure leaning out of the window, dressed in a cowl, and making signs to her. A friend who slept in this room found that lighted candles went out, and heard rustling round his bed all night.

The story, continued by the vicar, tells that the kneeling body of a woman had been found walled-up in the priests' room of Monkton Church quite recently. He then related:

"One day a tall young man, who said his name was Nordin, a medical student from Stockholm, approached me. He told me that more than 1,000 years ago his Viking ancestors came to Monkton, and that he was born there. When I took him to the top of the church tower, he pointed out to me places where, he said, he 'remembered' there used to be walls. We investigated and found, for the first time, that there certainly had been walls where he said they had existed. He recognised the old hall at once, told me where and how it had been altered, all quite accurately. In the old days, he said, it was a nunnery."

The vicar added that he believed the walled-up woman to be a nun whose spirit had been kept earthbound, because she had committed some sin. He conjectured that it could have been her task to wake the other nuns for a four o'clock service, and that she would continue to do so until an exorcism took place.

Vikings did visit this area in the past and Nordin told the vicar that he had saved up for years to visit Monkton, which he said he remembered after 1,000 years!

Before the days of modern medicine, charming took place to effect a cure, and this was practised until fairly recent times in the Tenby district. One practitioner, known locally as "The Charmer", as told by Gwynn Jones in his "Welsh Folklore", waved her hands about while she plaited straws, and said the words: "From the crown of the head to the sole of thy foot, may the Lord heal thee". This was accompanied by mumbling, and the patient was told that, as The Charmer already possessed faith, the sufferer did not need to have any himself! One of the visits had to be made on a Sunday and, as a result, people queued on that day while waiting for their turn to see The Charmer. Rickety children were not taken to a doctor, but to a wise woman, who charmed for them, this charm consisting of an incision made on a part of the ear, with the recital of an incantatory formula, and the superstition survived until fairly recently.

A local cure for warts was to rub them with fat black snails, after which the snail was placed on a bramble bush with the thorns piercing its body. The warts disappeared when the snail putrefied.

Vervain, with its semi-mystical associations, was highly regarded. The steam from the boiled leaves was inhaled to prevent fevers, and a drink made was said to be an effective cure for "many ill humours". There is a connection with the medicinal use of grass here, for the grass in St. Edryn's Churchyard was said to be a definite remedy for hydrophobia, and was used for curing people as well as animals.

There are gruesome legends connected with death and disability, which survived into the present century. One Pembrokeshire woman denied having made a certain statement and said that, if she was telling a lie, the child she was carrying would be born blind and that there would be a blind child in the succeeding nine generations. The narrator of this story had seen four generations, each with its blind child.

Belief in witchcraft still lingers on in parts of the country, and some families are thought to inherit magic powers. They are treated with caution and suspicion, and it is dangerous to offend them. An ancient tradition stated that descendants of those who had eaten eagle's flesh were able to cure shingles, but this statement is due to an error, as the Welsh word for shingles is "eryr" or eagle.

Many elderly women were accused of being witches, and illness or ill-luck was put down to an evil glance from the Black Witch. Such witches were often caught by making them sit on a chair, then sticking them through with a two-pronged fork. Shed teeth were thought to be especially vulnerable and had to be burned to prevent witches from using them as holders for spells.

In order to track down the actual witch responsible, names of all local witches were written on pieces of paper and placed, folded, into a bottle of urine. This was shaken and emptied out, the first name emerging being that of the culprit. A barbaric witch-hunt then took place, with the searchers armed with knives and other implements to force a confession. If the witch confessed, a fine was levied upon her and, if she denied the charge, her clothes were torn off and blood was drawn. Such cruelties took place in remote parts of the country.

Edward Laws says that Pembrokeshire witches were not usually malevolent. According to his story, when H.M.S. "Lion" was launched at Pembroke Dock in the 1840's, an old woman demanded admission into the reserved seats, which was refused. She retaliated to this insult by saying "Then there will be no launch today; you may all go home, good people" and departed. The "Lion" was named, her bows besprinkled with wine, the dogshores were knocked away, but the vessel never moved, nor was she got off until the spring tides came round again.

"Witches Butter" was the name given to a fungus which grew on old rafters and cowsheds. There was a superstition that, if this fell on any animal and clung to its back, that animal would die; therefore, farmers regarded this fungus with dread.

Every cow on the farm was christened, when turned out of its pen for the first time. The farmer, or his eldest daughter, would give grass to the calf, which was sprinkled with salt at the same time as the name was given. The names of cows were always Welsh, whereas dogs and horses were almost always given English names.

The cure for bewitchment in the 1850's was the same as that of the previous century. Finger-nail parings of the bewitched person were thrown into the fire, while a near relative of the afflicted person stood near an open window. The witch would then be seen approaching in great agony and, seeing the look-out, would ask:

"How is so-and-so?"

The answer, "Very bad today", would bring the reply from the witch:

"Poor thing, God bless her then".

Immediately, the bewitched person was said to become strong again.

In days of perilous travel, it took eight horses to pull the Carmarthen coach up the craggy ascent of the old road out of Tenby, according to G. Huntingdon, Rector of Tenby in his "Random Recollections". When pitch-dark country roads had to be negotiated on foot, it would not have been surprising to see a headless carriage rushing past, or to meet the Grey Lady riding her spectral mare near the ruins of Scotsborough and Trefloyne.

South Gate from St. George St.

10

Seasonal Customs

1. Christmas

Each season of the year kept its own special traditions, which stemmed from a time when most people worked in agriculture, depending on the seasons and using basic skills to earn their living. The old religious festivals were replaced by Christian worship, which laid a veneer over the old pagan symbolism, and from that time Christmas and Easter became the main times for ritual and celebration.

In Tenby, large crowds collected on Christmas Eve, and paraded through the streets in procession, carrying lighted torches which "flowed about in a manner that threatened at times the whole town - a fire-engine being then as now unknown in Tenby", according to an article "Manners and Customs of the People of Tenby in the eighteenth century, reprinted from the "Cambrian Journal", September 1857.

"Cow-horns racked the listening ears", and verses were shouted, beginning 'Christmas comes but once a year', while the Christmas chimes rang out. Private houses had previously decorated their windows with a "variety of quaint devices, formed of leaves of evergreens, mainly box, myrtle or holly - with its red berries - and few places were seen without these Christmas symbols".

At four o'clock on Christmas Day, the young men of the town called at the Rector's residence to escort him to Church. They put out their torches in the porch and went in to the early morning service. Everyone took candles to light the Church, as it was too dark otherwise to read the Service! Carols followed the prayers, and each year local poets wrote special new ones, some of which were extremely long, and which were all written in the traditional metres. Two or three hundred coloured candles were placed on the communion table, pulpit, window sills and pews. Church and Chapel people went to this service together. When the service ended, torches were relighted, the procession returned to the Rectory, the chimes continuing to ring until the time of the usual morning service. The Welsh work "Plygain" means "the morning light".

Before the service, the young people held parties at which they made treacle toffee from an old recipe and, after the service, the men went squirrel hunting and then on to football matches. This was a great day for visiting friends and family, and also for making up old quarrels. All debts were supposed to be paid off at Christmas. Poor people, going from door to door, were rarely sent away empty.

For the previous fortnight, the "waits" went on their nightly rounds and on Christmas Eve the postman, who was decked out with ribbons, went about asking for the customary Christmas box.

In contrast, two savage ceremonies took place on St. Stephen's Day, or Boxing Day. The first was the barbarous and cruel custom of "holly beating". In this, a furious onslaught was made by men and boys, armed with prickly holly, on the naked arms of female servants. Their short-sleeved jackets made them an easy prey to this beating, and their bleeding arms showed the severity of the attacks. This practice is said to stem from the martyrdom of St. Stephen on December 26th, but the ritual died out when a police force became established.

The second ceremony was the hunting of the wren. The cutty, or diminutive, wren, who was the enemy of the robin, was hunted with sticks and staves in bushes and woodland on St. Stephen's Day. As soon as it flew upwards, it was ritually killed by one of the men who was then pronounced "King". Only on this day was the wren allowed to be hunted and, should it be molested on any other day of the year, rashes and burning weals would inflict the intruder.

In Tenby, the wren was captured and placed in a small ornamented box, or paper house, with a square of glass at each end. One of these wren houses, from Marloes in Pembrokeshire, can be seen in St. Fagan's Folk Museum outside Cardiff. The house was decorated with coloured ribbons.

The name "drwy" by which the wren is known in Wales, suggests a druidic origin, and the wren was supposed to influence the course of justice by whispering the verdict at courts of law in the druid's ear. It was a bird associated with thunder and the oaktree. The bright flash of colour on the goldcrest's breast (usually called a "wren"), was thought to be the last ray of the dying sun at the time of the winter solstice, the shortest day of the year.

Two or four men would carry the little wren house on four long poles, pretending that it was very heavy indeed, and at the same time singing a long repetitive song. The men would then go into houses and sing for beer money. This song had ten stanzas, the first one being as follows:

> "O where are you going? says Milder to Malder,
> O where are you going? says the younger to the elder;
> O I cannot tell, says Festel to Fose.
> We're going to the woods, says John the Red Nose,
> We're going to the woods, says John the Red Nose."

The song continued monotonously, saying that the hunters were going to shoot the Cutty Wren with bows and arrows, then with great guns and cannons, bringing her home on four strong men's shoulders, or on big carts and wagons. They were going to cut her up with knives and forks, hatchets and cleavers, and boil her in pots and kettles, or brass pans and cauldrons.

With the wren house, it was usual to enter the house of newly-weds, who had been married for less than one year, and to sprinkle them with well water. Each house doorstep entered was marked with white chalk, to keep out evil spirits and to show that gifts had been received.

The body, or feather, of a wren was said to be a talisman against shipwreck for one year, and this was much sought after by local fishermen to take out in their boats. Sometimes the bird was plucked and roasted, probably because of the horrible martyrdom of St. Stephen on a gridiron.

When the bearers were very drunk, the wren's body was buried on the dunghill heap, the most abominated place in the town, but as days grew longer the bright flash of the bird's breast would be resurrected with the returning sun.

For three weeks before and after Christmas, the Christmas mummers, or "guisers" went round, mostly in threes, in a quaint costume, visiting every house. When admitted, they held dialogues in doggerel rhyme and, when in Tenby, told a story of how St. George came to the town to fight a Turk! This was not as far-fetched as it sounds today, for in the seventeenth century, Barbary corsairs, who were locally called "Turks", sailed up the Channel and sometimes attacked a village, carrying off its unwary inhabitants into slavery.

Each of the three mummers represented various characters, and they are numbered in the following verses as 1, 2 and 3, and quoted from "Tales and Traditions of Tenby":

No.1. "Here comes I, old Father Christmas
Christmas or not,
I hope old Father Christmas
Will never be forgot.
A room - make room here gallant boys
And give us room to rhyme,
We're come to show activity
Upon a Christmas time.
Acting youth or acting age
The like was never acted on the stage;
If you don't believe what I now say
Enter St. George and clear the way".

No.2. "Here comes I, St. George the valiant man,
With naked sword and spear in hand,
Who fought the dragon, and
brought him to the slaughter
And for this won the King of Egypt's *daughter
What man or mortal will dare to stand
Before me with my sword in hand;
I'll slay him, and cut him as small as flies,
And send him to Jamaica to make mince pies."

* Occasionally King of England's daughter

St. George's challenge is soon taken up:

No.3. "Here comes I, a Turkish knight,
In Turkish land I learned to fight
I'll fight St. George with courage bold,
And if his blood's hot, will make it cold."

No.2 answers:
"If thou are a Turkish knight,
Draw out thy sword, and let us fight."

In the resulting battle, the Turk falls and St. George, struck with remorse exclaims:

> "Ladies and gentlemen,
>   You've seen what I've done,
> I've cut the Turk down
>   Like the evening sun;
> Is there a doctor that can be found,
>   To cure this knight of his deadly wound?"

No. 1 re-enters, changed:

> "Here comes I, a doctor,
>   A ten pound doctor;
> I've a little bottle in my pocket,
>   Called hokum, skokum, alicompane;
> I'll touch his eyes, nose, mouth and chin,
>   And say 'rise dead man' and he'll fight again."

After touching the prostrate Turk, he leaps up ready again for the battle. St. George, however, thinks this to be an opportunity to sound his own praises:

> "Here am I, St. George with shining armour bright,
>   I am a famous champion, also a worthy knight;
> Seven long years in a close cave was kept,
>   And out of that into a prison leaped,
> From out of that with a rock of stones
>   There I laid down my grievious bones.
> Many a giant did I subdue
>   And run a fiery dragon through
> I fought the man of Tillotree,
>   And still will gain the victory
> First, then, I fought in France,
>   Second, I fought in Spain,
> *Thirdly I came to Tenby*
>   *To fight the Turk again.*"

After a fight, St. George again overcomes the Turk and asks for a doctor, who again makes a miraculous cure and comes forward as the Protector:

> "Here comes I, Oliver Cromwell,
>   As you may suppose,
> Many nations I have conquered
>   With my copper nose.
> I made the French tremble,
>   And the Spanish for to quake,
> I fought the jolly Dutchman,
>   And made their hearts to ache."

No. 2. then becomes Satan:

> "Here comes I, Beelzebub,
>   And under my arm I carry a club,
> Under my chin I carry a pan,
>   Don't I look a nice young man?"

No. 3 then hints at the purpose of the visit:

> "Ladies and gentlemen,
>   Our story is ended,
> Our money box is recommended,
>   Five or six shillings will not do us harm,
> Silver, or copper, or gold if you can."

After the response to this appeal, st. George, the Turk, Doctor, Oliver Cromwell, and Beelzebub all leave the house.

11

Seasonal Customs

2. New Year and Twelfth Night

In Pembrokeshire, to rise early on New Year's Day would ensure good luck for the coming year. It was unlucky to do any work on this day, and people went out early to obtain a fresh loaf to bring into the house. No female visitor was allowed to cross the threshold until a man or boy had crossed it first.

There was a general desire to see the Old Year out and the New Year in. Some people danced the Old Year out, some sang it out, drank it out, a few prayed it out, but very many walked it out. The promenaders sung verses like the following, somewhat unharmoniously:

"Get up on New Year's morning,
The cocks are all a-crowing;
And if you think you're awake too soon
Why get up and look at the stars and moon,
But get up on New Year's morning".

Children used to go round singing for pennies or cakes, chanting as they did near Tenby:

"The roads are very dirty,
My shoes are very thin,
I wish you a happy New Year
And please to let me in".

This took place so that anyone was still asleep should be woken up promptly!

By far the best known Tenby custom is the ceremony of New Year Water. Very early in the morning, boys and girls would fill an earthenware cup, or a tin, with spring water, drawn fresh that day from the well. A bunch of evergreens, such as box, myrtle, rosemary or sea spurge would be dipped into the water and used to sprinkle the hands and faces of everyone they met. When one of these children was admitted to the house, every room from kitchen to attic would also be sprinkled. The fee would range from copper to silver coins, and snatches of song would be sung duriing the ceremony.

The Reverend J. B. Smith, who was a curate at Tenby, took down this verse from Tenby children, and it is quoted from the Archaeologia Cambrensis for 1848 (page 141), but has some variations:

"Here we bring new water from the well so clear,
For to worship God with, this happy New Year,
Sing levy dew, sing levy dew, the water and the wine,
With seven bright gold wires, and bugles that do shine;
Sing reign of fair maid, with gold upon her toe,
Open you the west door, and turn the Old Year go
Sing reign of fair maid, with gold upon her chin,
Open you the east door, and let the New Year in".

"Levy dew" appears to be an English version of "Llef i Dduw" or "llef ar Dduw", i.e. in Welsh "a cry to God". The verses are probably of pagan origin, and the sprinkling a survival of the use of Holy Water.

A decorated apple or orange was also carried round, and called a "rhodd calenig". This was put on the mantlepiece until it withered. The fruit was decorated with oats, wheat and barley and a sprig of holly. It stood on a small tripod of three skewers. There was competition for the best decorated one, and gifts were given to the children who carried it.

Twelfth Night used to be kept as a time of wassail and revelry. Towards dusk, many people from the town and neighbourhood walked from house to house with their "wassail bowls". This name came from the Saxon custom of drinking health, when the words "waes-hael" or "health be to you" were said in greeting.

Those who drank from the wassail bowls were expected to pay, and a very long song was sung on this occasion. The two verses quoted are first, an invitation to the wassail, while the second one shows the consequence of accepting the invitation:

The Wassail Bowl

"Taste our jolly wassail bowl,
   Made of cake, apple, ale and spice,
Good master give command
   You shall taste once or twice
Of our jolly wassail bowl".

"Are there any maidens here,
   As I suppose there's none,
Or they wouldn't leave us here
   Freezing on the cold stone,
With our jolly wassail bowl".

On this same day, in rural districts rather than in the town, "tooling" took place. This was the practice of calling at different farmhouses, or wherever Sir John Barleycorn held his court, and pretending to look for one's tools behind the beer cask, giving a broad hint of the reason for this visit. A carpenter who said "I've left my saw behind your beer cask", was at once presented with a cup of beer.

"Souling" or "sowling" round wealthy neighbours, was the custom of demanding soul (or possibly soûl - French for "one's fill", or saouler - to satisfy with food), by poor women. This custom originally took place on St. Thomas's Day, December 21st. Any food which was eater with bread was begged, such as meat, fish and particularly cheese.

The Mari Lwyd was mainly associated with Monmouthshire and Glamorganshire, but was also practised in Pembrokeshire. A horse's head was made by draping a large white cloth or canvas sheet over a horse's skull; alternatively, a sheet was sewn up to make the horse's head shape. The eyes were made of large buttons, gloves were used for ears, and a man with a pitchfork stood under the sheet moving the horse's head. This spectre was taken round houses and pushed in through the windows, considerably frightening those inside. A Tenby resident recently told the author how terrified his mother used to be of the Mari Lwyd. The Twelfth Night wassailers, who went round with this apparition were ornamented and decked out with ribbons, but the origin of this custom is still unknown.

Until 1936, when Welsh racing went into decline, National Hunt racing took place at New Hedges during the winter months, when Dick Rees was the local idol.

The modern thriller writer, once a jockey himself, Dick Francis, was born near Tenby in 1920.

12

Seasonal Customs

3. Easter and Whitsun

St. David's Day, March 1st, was the first occasion in the New Year for another celebration. Members of one of the benefit clubs marched through the town of Tenby with a leek in their hats. In the evening, a ball took place, and at this function expensive artificial leeks were worn by the men and women. This practice had been discontinued by 1856.

On Old St. David's Day, which was the 12th March, it was the custom in farmhouses to place a wooden candle, instead of a tallow one, in the candlestick on the table. This "canwyll-bren" was a sign that the evening meal would no longer be taken in artificial light by the farm workers. Candles were then valuable items and people went to bed very early.

Shrove Tuesday was usually divided between kicking a football and eating pancakes. Shop windows were shuttered, and private houses in the main streets barricaded their windows with laths, bags and sacking. About noon, with a rush and yell, some two or three hundred Tenbyonians would go past, kicking, hooting, shouting, wrestling, "in one chaotic mass, the ball meanwhile flying upwards kicked by the players' feet", according to "Tales and Traditions of Tenby".

The game of cnapan, perhaps the first Welsh Rugby football, was played in rural districts in Elizabethan times, and it is thought to have originated with the Trojans or Ancient Britons. This was played with a ball made of box wood, yew, crab or holly, boiled in tallow to make it slippery, and called a cnapan. It was hurled bolt upright into the air and, when caught, was thrown towards the part of the country for which the catcher played. The play was not over until the ball had been sent too far to return it that night. There was no "goal" in this game.

Sometimes the play was followed by a thousand or fifteen hundred naked men, for any clothing worn would have been torn to shreds. There were also fore-runners, or scouts, who had to keep in front of the cnapan wherever it was passed, and who were on the opposite side of the other party and "home". The main body of players would cry out "Cadwol", i.e. "Look well to their backs".

Horsemen also took part, carrying cudgels three and a half feet long, with which they struck the other horsement to get them to give up the cnapan. The foot men were only allowed to use their bare fists, and while the horsemen were not allowed to go among the barefooted troops, the footmen could hurl stones at the horsemen to keep them away. The players came home with broken heads, bruises and black faces.

As well as football kicking, several fights took place in the churchyard with "other gymnastic recreations". When these ended towards evening, the town became its usual peaceful place again.

When Good Friday arrived, three old traditions had a strong hold on Tenby people. Until the end of the eighteenth century, the old people used to walk barefoot to church "so as not to disturb the earth", which was a custom from pre-Reformation times. An old woman, named Martha Evans, who was alive in the mid-nineteenth century, remarked the difference between those days and the time when, in her youth, all business was suspended, no horse or cart was seen in the town, and the barefoot custom prevailed.

After the Church service, hot cross buns were eaten, but a certain number of them were tied up in a bag and hung in the kitchen. They were kept there until the following Good Friday, when they were replaced, not before time! Pieces of these buns were used as a cure for any person or animal who became ill and who was then given a piece of the bun to eat. They were also thought to protect the house and family from evil spirits, and the animals from disease.

Young people would meet together and go down to the fields of South Pembrokeshire, the "Englishry", where they collected long reed leaves from the river and wove them into the shape of a man. This figure was then laid on a wooden cross and placed in a little-used part of a field or garden, where it was left. This was referred to as "making Christ's bed", and may have been derived from an old and popular Popish custom of burying an image of Christ on Good Friday. Brand, in his "Popular Antiquities", quotes a German author, who referred in 1600 to the same custom:

"An other image doe they get, like one but newly deade,
With legges stretcht out at length, and hands upon his body spreade,
And him, with pompe and sacred song, they beare unto his grave."

On Easter morning, people climbed a local hill to "see the sun dance". On Easter Even, or Easter Tuesday, a girl was crowned with a circular crown made of earthenware, which had points forming cups, each filled with a drink. Candles were stuck on with clay between the cups, and you had to drink without getting burned, or burning the girl.
There was an Easter custom of ball playing in St. Mary's Churchyard, against the Church walls. Tennis balls were also thrown over the church roof. Dancing used to take place in many churchyards at this season, and this is thought to be the remnant of an ancient druidic rite, which took place inside a sacred circle of yew trees.
Easter Monday was given over to merrymaking, and many people went over to the neighbouring village of Gumfreston, "where some amused themselves with the barbarous sport of cock-fighting". Others went to the two tea-parties held annually at Tenby and Gumfreston, which were known as the "Parish Clerk's Meeting", or "The Parish Clerk's Ale", where drinking, and dancing to the fiddler took place.
The following story is told of two Tenby characters:
"George Langdon and Tommy Jacks, two poor men, were well-known characters in the town in the early 1800's. Both were objects of charity, and George, though born blind, was shrewd and could act as a guide to strangers; on dark nights, lantern in hand, he led the way through narrow, steep streets, never failing to take 'the strange captain' to his own ship in the harbour.
"He was the favourite messenger of the townspeople, thus gaining a few pence, and also 'the fiddler' sought after on Easter Mondays and Whit Mondays, when the servants attended 'the Ales', each paying the musicians two or three pence, and dancing an unlimited time to the blind fiddler's merry tunes.
"But the fiddler became very jealous of his rival in the penny gifts as Tommy, being an imbecile, had many kind friends who bestowed their mite on him. The blind man, in order to be rid of his rival, enticed him to a low part of the wall near the Gun Fort, and had nearly succeeded in forcing him over the cliff, when a sailor came to the rescue of poor Tommy."
Maying time was the holiday season most enjoyed by Tenby people, for

everyone was able to join in the celebrations. On May Eve, the inhabitants all turned out carrying boughs of hawthorn in full bloom, which were also decorated with flowers and placed outside house windows.

Hall's "Guide to Tenby" describes the King and Queen of May who "tricked out with flowers, paraded the town and demanded from all candles - or money wherewith to buy - which were to be used at night for illuminating the May-bush, round which dancing was kept up while the lights lasted". An immense bonfire of furze was then lighted, on which the May-bush was burned.

Maypoles were reared up in different parts of the town, decorated with flowers, coloured papers and bunches of variegated ribbon. May Eve was once the day when the druidical spring sacrifices, preceding May Day, took place. These sacrifices were originally human, and later animal, and they were made on huge bonfires or, it is believed, with the victims immolated in wicker cages.

On May Day, young men and girls, hand in hand, would dance round the maypoles and "thread the needle". A group of from fifty to one hundred would dance their way from one pole to another, until they had crossed the town. Meeting other similar groups, the parties would form a "lady and chain" on their way. The maypoles were carefully guarded by a "watch", for it was the custom to try to pull down other poles set up. The maypoles belonged to the children of several localities in which they were erected, and the parents would often mount guard to repel invaders. Sometimes a surprise attack took place, when both parties joined in the joke in a friendly way. If a piece of hawthorn in flower was found broken off in the road, it was never picked up, for this was fatal to anyone who claimed it.

Whitsun was a riotous time, when large parties visited Caldey Island for rabbit and puffin shooting. Much drinking took place and picnics followed the shooting. The boatmen and revellers were not always in a sober condition when returning to the mainland in their small boats!

On Whit Monday, a women's benefit club walked in procession to Church, preceded by a band and banners, carrying bunches of flowers in their hands.

After the service, they dined and finished off the evening by dancing "Sir Roger de Coverley", "John Saunders" and other popular dances to the accompaniment of a fiddler.

On St. Peter's Day, June 29th, poor folk in Pembrokeshire used to go about begging for butter instead of alms. They carried this in a type of jug which was called "the jug of Peter's butter".

13

Seasonal Customs

4. Harvest and Hollowe'en

At harvest time, the hayfield was a place to be avoided. Customs were boisterous, and anyone who entered the field was immediately pounced upon by haymakers of the opposite sex, tossed about on the hay and bound with bands. The victim was then blackmailed until a fine had been paid. This ceremony, when performed on women, was called "giving them a green gown", and when men were seized it was called "stretching their backs". This ritual respected neither age nor condition, according to "Tales and Traditions of Tenby".

In another account of this custom, the ceremony only took place on the day when the hay was carted into the hay yard. It was strictly reserved for young men and unmarried girls. A story is told of one occasion in 1905 when an old married woman called to another woman: "This is a funny how-de-do no'gring-grown'", as there were no women in the harvest field, "come on, you women, let's give Peter a 'gring grown', otherwise this land will never be fruitful again". It appears from this that the tradition sprang from an ancient fertility rite.

When the grain was brought to the mill to be ground, a celebration took place by young people of the district, which lasted all night. A horse's head was dressed up and taken around by night. Anyone the workmen found disagreeable was annoyed as much as possible.

The last sheaf of corn cut in Pembrokeshire became the "Wrach". All the reapers threw their sickles at it, and the one who succeeded in cutting the corn down was given a jug of home-brewed ale. It was usually the ploughman who made the Wrach from this sheaf. The person in charge of the Wrach had to be very careful to avoid observation, and took it to the neighbouring farm without the reapers finding out his errand. When within an easy distance of these neighbouring reapers, he would throw the Wrach over the fence, if possible upon the foreman's sickle. Then, taking to his heels, he would be lucky if he escaped without being caught by the flying sickles of the angry reapers, which they hurled after him.

Often the Wrach was taken into the house by one of the reapers, but this had to be done without any water touching it. The possessor of it was sometimes stripped of his clothing and deluged with water from buckets kept for this purpose. If, at last, the Wrach was taken into the farmhouse successfully, the bearer was paid a small fine by the master of the house, or given a jug of special beer, which was taken from a cask containing the best beer reserved for honoured visitors. The Wrach was then hung up on a nail from one of the beams, and this custom still exists in some rural areas.

St. Crispin's Day is the 25th October, and on the previous night, an effigy was made and hung up on some prominent place in the town of Tenby, such as the Church steeple. It was cut down on the morning of the 25th and carried around the town. At the same time, doggerel verses were read, which were supposed to be the Last Will and Testament of the Saint. All the items of clothing on the effigy were taken off and distributed to the different shoemakers, for St. Crispin and St. Crispinian, two brothers, were the patron saints of shoemakers. At last, nothing remained of the image except the padding, and this was kicked about by the crowds until it disintegrated.

In revenge for this treatment of St. Crispin, his followers hung up the effigy of a carpenter on St. Clement's Day, the 23rd November. This received the same treatment as before. St. Clement was the third Bishop of Rome after the Apostles, c.100 A.D.

It was the custom on this evening for the owners of fishing-boats to give a special supper to their crews, which consisted of roast goose and rice pudding.

Superstitions came to the fore, as the days grew shorter and the nights became darker and longer. Witchcraft, spell-binding and divination were all practised. The glance of a witch could bewitch a person or animal, it was thought, and the "evil eye" was much dreaded. Young women practised the various forms of divination to find out who would be their future husbands.

It was said that some people had made compacts with Satan who, when the contract expired, took away the victim, and left behind only a smell of sulphur. There were tales of opened coffins, which only contained stones, a reference to vampires. It was believed that the corpse of John Meyrick, Chief Justice of South Wales from Bush House, had been carried off by the Devil. So concerned was one elderly man living at Carew, as he had led a dissolute life, that he put a special clause in his Will. This insisted that he should be cremated, and his ashes riddled through a sieve from the top of Carew Church, so that the Devil should not claim him! His descendants did not carry out these final instructions.

After Bonfire Night, the old winter calends and now Guy Fawkes night, when the fire had burned out, there was a scramble home for fear of the Hwch Ddu Gwta, or the Tail-less Black Sow:
"A Black Sow without a tail,
And a White lady without a head:
May the Tail-less Black Sow snatch the hindmost.
On Winter's Eve a Black Sow without a tail,
And thieves coming along and knitting stockings".

Pigs were passed through bonfires to put a magical protection between them and the powers of evil which were abroad on that night.

All Hallows Eve with its customs, at the time of the year when the living and the dead became very close to each other, led up to the Christmas preparations, completing the cycle of seasons and their traditions.

North Beach

14

The Sea Serjeants
A Secret Society ·

Fenton, in his history of Pembrokeshire, says that this Society was revived in 1726 by the gentlemen of South Wales, for the purpose of spending a week happily together once a year. Their meetings were held in rotation in various seaports, and the number of members was not allowed to exceed twenty-five.

The Society met at Tenby on June 2nd 1753, when it elected Richard Gwynne of Taliaris as President. The last surviving member, John Harries of Presceli, died at the beginning of the nineteenth century.

Sir John Philipps, who was parliamentary candidate for the city of Bristol, was accused in 1754 of being the Chief of a secret Society, and he admitted that this was true. He stated in his defence that the Society was "composed of gentlemen of the first rank and fortune in Wales; Gentlemen who are as good as well affected subjects as any in His Majesty's dominions, and whose delight it always will be to see a great Prince, and a free and flourishing people, mutually striving to render each other happy. The intent, indeed, of our annual meeting is to spent a week together in innocent mirth and recreation, as other gentlemen do in England at a horse race, and for no disloyal purpose whatsoever".

Gentlemen wishing to become members were obliged to continue as probationers for at least one year before they could be admitted, in case of a vacancy, to participate in the full degree of serjeant; such was the caution they observed in the choice of their members. They had a president, a secretary, an examiner and two stewards. When there was a call of serjeants, that is, on their admission, they were to attend in their coifs and proper habit of the order, unless the president should dispense with the same. A silver star, with the figure of a dolphin in the centre, was to be worn as a characteristic badge on the coat by every member during the week of their meeting. "And that there might be no suspicion of their want of gallantry, they came to a resolution in the year 1749 to elect a lady patroness, an unmarried lady of the town or neighbourhood of their meeting, and that, as soon as elected, the secretary waited on her with the badge of the society".

The members, chaplain and probationers were each allowed to introduce a lady to attend the lady patroness to dine with the society one day in the week. Every member heard to curse or swear during the meeting in the public room incurred a penalty. This also applied to every person who should presume to play at dice, and who was fined five guineas. "In short", continues Fenton, "all their rules and orders for the internal economy of the society, which were numerous, evince great good sense, consideration and propriety and seem well calculated to promote elegant festivity, restrain the exuberance of youthful spirit, and to prevent the excess of social joy degenerating into profanation, vice and riot".

They had some striking regulations, "which to have formed, did them honour as men of humanity and British subjects in general, and as Welshmen in particular, sufficient to silence the calumny thrown out against them by the cold-blooded and invidious, who condemn every sort of association that springs from sensibilities they are strangers to, and is not cemented by some sordid interest or other".

The examination undergone by each member on being admitted was dignified and simple, and is given by Fenton from the last examiner's original manuscript:

Modus Examinandi
(A Greek sub-title is added)

"Do you bear true allegiance to His Majesty?

"Are you a member of the Church of England as by law established?

"Will you be faithful to your friends in prosperity, and cherish them in adversity?

"Do you desire to be a member of this Society?

"Will you faithfully observe the rules and orders that have been read to you?

"Will you, upon the honour of a gentleman, keep the secrets of the Society, and the form of your admission into it?

In writing to each other "they always subscribed themselves brothers, and by all accounts there never was a more united fraternity".

Ancient Building on Harbour

15

Old Tenby, the Market and St. Margaret's Fair

The origin of Tenby lies buried in mystery. A "fine fortress on the ninth wave" is mentioned in the ninth century poem from the Book of Taliesin "Etmic Dinbych" or "Praise of Tenby". In this poem, the anonymous bard describes his patron, a lord of Dyfed named Bleiddudd, who has died and "gone to the oaken church". He mentions the crying white seagulls above the splendid fort with waves beating against the rocks, while feasting and revelry take place.

This poem contains many obscurities, which scholars are still unravelling. There is a possible reference to Caldey Island in the "cell" mentioned in the penultimate stanza, where the poet stayed, and a privilege or "braint" to the men of Tenby has been referred to in connection with the "rights" mentioned. The feasting may refer to a wake at Calends, or a festival at New Year. North Walians are not shown in a good light! It has also been put forward that the chief court of Dyfed may have been at Tenby, rather than Narberth. Anthony Conran's poem, in translation from the Welsh original, is printed at the end of this chapter.

This fortress at Tenby is not heard of again until the twelfth century, when an incident took place at Amroth, then called Earweare, which is on the far side of Monkton Point next to Saundersfoot, across the sands of Carmarthen Bay.

Here there was a castle "a fair place belonging to the Eliottes", where Cadwgan ap Blethin, who was married to the daughter of a Norman chief, had his residence. After Cadwgan's death, Cadell, the son of Grufydd ap Rhys, took possession of it as a hunting seat, and it was in this neighbourhood, in the forest of Coedtraeth above Saundersfoot, "while he was out hunting only with a small retinue, the men of Tenby lay in ambush for him and, having put to flight his unarmed attendants, wounded the prince so dangerously that he narrowly escaped with life".

John Leland, the earliest modern English antiquary, who toured the Principality between 1534 and 1543, continues this story by telling us that the two brothers of Cadell, in revenge, attacked the castle of Tenby in 1150 after a march at night over the sands from Amroth. He also describes Tenby:

"Tenbigh Town stondeth on a main rokke, but not veri hy, and the Severn Se so gulfeth in about hit, that at the ful se almost the third parte of the toune is inclosid with water. The towne is strongly waullid and well gatid, everi gate having his portcolis "ex solido ferro . . . in the middes of the toune is a faire paroche chirch".

In another version of the atack on Tenby, Richard Fenton in his "Pembrokeshire" (1810) goes further and says that "having surprised the castle unobserved, they put the garrison to the sword and, after destroying a great part of the town by fire, decamped without hurt".

Since that date, Amroth has suffered great damage by erosion. A submerged forest was discovered on the beach, after the sand had been washed away in storms. A new road was made to replace the east village road which vanished, and a row of cottages on the seaward side of the village disappeared completely. Today, it would be impossible to walk to Amroth across the sands, and the considerable change of level in beach and foreshore in the area of Tenby is dealt with in a later chapter.

After the first attack on Tenby by Meredith and Rhys in 1150, when William Fitzgerald was Governor of the Castle, nearly a third of the town lay in ruins. In 1187 the town was sacked by Maelgwn, the warlike son of "Lord" Rhys ap Gruffydd, and again in 1260 by the Welsh prince, Llewellyn ap Gruffydd.

Pembrokeshire had been constantly under siege from invaders. Roman power lasted for 320 years, and the Romans are said to have built two towns in the county, Menapia or Old St. David's, and Caer Alun, which is Haverfordwest. Tenby may have been either a small naval station or a health resort, but evidence is lacking. Coins relating to the whole Roman rule in Britain have been found, of Vespasian, Marcus Aurelius, Faustina, Probus, Maximinus, Carausius, Constantine, Constantine II, and Constans. But the strangest coin was found at the Esplanade in 1880 and was a Graeco-Bactrian coin of the 2nd century B.C.!

At the end of the eight century, Scandinavians began to raid the coast, making twenty-one attacks between 795 and 1157. They settled in Pembroke and left many Viking names in the area.

The name Dinbych, which eventually became Tenby, probably came into being in Romano-British times, or even earlier than this. The name is first mentioned in the Laws of Hywel dda (Howell the Good), which were certified at Whitland. As early as 1245 AD. the name "Tinbye" was both written and spoken much as it is today. There are more than sixty variations of the name. Tynbye, Tinby, Tenbye and Tenby were used in the 17th and 18th centuries, the last being stabilised and used today.

In 1106, as the result of great flooding, the Flemish dykes were destroyed and Henry I offered the Flemings, who were now homeless, a settlement in Wales. In 1135, a second contingent of Flemings came to Pembrokeshire under Henry II and it is thought small groups established themselves at Angle and Tenby. They were ruthless colonists, but they did not take over the whole of Pembrokeshire, and they did not get on well with the Norman military aristocracy of Dyfed. Mainly mercenary soldiers and "a people well versed in commerce and woollen manufactories," they were, according to Giraldus Cambrensis, "a people anxious to seek gain by sea or land in defiance of fatigue and danger, a hardy race equally fitted for plough or sword, a brave and happy people". Large numbers of Englishmen came into South Dyfed until the end of the 13th century, mostly from the West Country, gradually overwhelming the Flemings.

In 1523-4, Cardinal Wolsey received a letter from one R. Gruffithe, which said:

"There is so gret aboundance of Irisshemen lately comyn within these twelve months into Pembrokeshire ... And the king's towne of Tenbye is almost clean Irisshe, as the hedde men and rulers, as the comyns of the sayde towne, and of their high and presumptuous myndes do dissobey all maner the king's pocesse that comethe to them out of the King's Exchequer of Pembroke. And one of them called Germyn Gruffithe born under the great dominion of the said Erle is now owner of two great ships well appointed with ordennances ..." (Letter dated VIII July).

G. Gruffithe became a Bailiff of Tenby in 1526.

In 1602, George Owen of Henllys (Lord of Cemaes 1552-1613), historian, said that every third, fourth or fifth householder was an Irishman, and that Irishmen ferried over to the country every day. These Irish people "made aqua vitie in great aboundance selling it through the country on horse-back". His report is said to be somewhat exaggerated.

The inhabitants of Pembrokeshire appear to have acquired a reputation for hard drinking early in the seventeenth century. Samuel Ward of Ipswich preached and published a sermon in 1627, which he called "The

Life of Faith in Death", in which numerous instances proving the ill-effects of drunkenness are cited, among others: "At Tenby in Pembrokeshire, a drunkard being exceedingly drunke broke himself all to pieces off an high steepe rock in a most fearful manner, and yet the occasion and circumstances of his fall so ridiculous, as I think not fit to relate, lest in so serious a judgement I should move laughter to the reader".

As would be expected, a mixture of traditions is found in this so-called "Little England Beyond Wales", Welsh and Irish customs, English and Flemish influences remaining to this day.

When the Slebech estate, situated by the side of the East Cleddau river near Haverfordwest, was granted to Colonel Horton in 1645, the Officers of his regiment were given an interest in this property. Among these was a Captain Richard Castle, who took up residence in Narberth Castle, and who proceeded to establish a market.

"This was a great grievance to the inhabitants of Tenby who, by right of their Charter, claimed a monopoly of fairs and markets in the Hundred" states Edward Laws. It was thought that Narberth would take away their business.

"During the Commonwealth, Tenby people fearing that Captain Castle would have an ear of the Court, hesitated to move over this but, soon after the Restoration, prosecuted Captain Castle under a quo warranto. The defendant pleaded the general issue, there was judgement for the King and Castle was fined £100, but on submission and a promise to discontinue the market, this fine was remitted by Sir Samuel Diggs, one of the Justices for the Great Sessions of the County of Pembroke."

"In spite of this, Narberth market was not closed and in 1671 the Major, Alderman, Bailiffs, Burgesses and other inhabitants of Tenby instituted proceedings against Captain Castle." This memorable lawsuit lasted for five years, and there are twelve documents among the Corporation's archives referring to this suit, one of which is quoted below:

"It was represented to his Majesty that the Towne of Tenby do open their Markets at such unseasonable Hours, that those who resort thither with commodities are forced to undersell them, or tarry so late that in their return homewards they are in hazard of their lives by reason of the dangerous passages in the Dark among ye coal pits. Which Mischief His Majesty, desiring to have prevented out of his tender care for the Security of his Subjects hath thought fit, and doth hereby order and command that the Markets at Tenby be opened for the future at eleven o'clock in the morning at the latest".

In the end, Narberth Market was suppressed and Captain Richard Castle probably ruined. This was in 1676, but in the year 1688 the above

Order was rescinded and Narberth obtained a grant for a market and fairs. In spite of the order made in 1676, a market was held at Narberth every Wednesday in the year 1684, four years before permission was obtained.

George Owen writes in a manuscript in the British Museum (Archaeologia Cambrensis 1850) that Tenby Market was held on Saturday for victuals and Wednesday for corn:

"Tenby, where there is a daylie markett thereof... and therefore it is in Welsh called Denbigh-y-Pysgod, that is fishe Tenby, for difference between it and Denbigh in North Wales".

St. Margaret's Fair used to be held under the town walls but, because of traffic and tourist congestion in the summer season, it has been moved to Butts Field. The fair lasts for three days and is held annually. It was formerly held in August, in accordance with the Royal Charter. There is a traditional colourful opening ceremony, with the procession including the Mayor, the Town Crier and the town band. There are stalls, sideshows, roundabouts and all the fun of the fair. At the opening, the Town Crier, with his bell, makes the following announcement:-

"This is to give notice that the fair is now open and will be held for three days by Royal Charter, and should any grievance arrive a court of 'pie poudre' will be held in the Town Hall, before the Mayor and Magistrates, to redress the same".

Today, when dusty feet (pie Poudre) are not as common as they were in Elizabethan times, this ancient court still sits, and anyone can appeal to it.

St. Margaret also giver her name to a small island, which is joined to Caldey Island by a reef of rocks, seen at low tide. The island used to be called "Little Caldey" in Elizabethan times.

Another annual activity was the Fire Brigade Carnival held on Castle Hill, and the Carnival still takes place today, with a procession through the town. An old notice informing people of this event reads:

"In pursuance of the powers conferred on the Local Authority by Section 44 of the Public Health Acts Amendment Act, 1890, the Castle Hill will be closed on August 7th 1929 from 5 p.m. on the occasion of the Fire Brigade Carnival. Admission to Hill Sixpence. By Order. G. Meyrick Price, Town Clerk, August 1st 1929."

(Printed by the Tenby Observer", Printing Works, Frog St. Tenby.)

Castle Hill was again closed on the occasion of the annual Tenby Regatta. In 1930 admission to this event was one shilling for adults and sixpence for children.

Copyright Anthony Conran.

The Penguin Book of Welsh Verse.1967
Reprinted by permission of Penguin Books Ltd.

PRAISE OF TENBY Anonymous c.875
Anthony Conran introduces the poem as follows:-
This has all the marks of being a "Dadolwch", or poem of reconciliation between a poet and his patron. The patron is a lord of Dyfed, or Pembrokeshire, called Bleiddudd; but the poem is remarkable among those of its type in that Bleiddudd is dead, 'gone to the oaken church', and the poet is making peace with his heir, the new head of Erbin's line, master of the 'little fort' - Dinbych or Tenby. If the last line of this translation is correct, which is open to doubt, it looks as though the poem was intended for recitation at Bleiddudd's funeral feast, as the November Calends, the festival of the beginning of winter. It is markedly anti-North Walian: Dyfed and Gwynedd must at this time have been at one another's throats. I have omitted the final couplet to God, and also a stray, fragmentary stanza that follows it in the manuscript.

> I ask for God's favour, saviour of the folk,
> Master of heaven and earth, greatly prudent and wise.
>
> There is a fine fortress stands on the sea,
> The bright headland is gay at the Calends,
> And when the ocean puts forth its might
> Commonly poets are loud over mead-cups.
> The hurrying wave surges against it,
> They abandon the green flood to the Picts.
> And through my prayer, O God, may I find
> As I keep faith, atonement with you.
>
> There is a fine fortress on the broad ocean,
> Unyielding stronghold, sea round its edge.
> Enquire, O Britain, who rightly owns it -
> Yours, head of Erbin's line, yours be it now!
> In this palisade were war-band and throng,
> Eagle in cloud on the track of pale faces:
> Before that lord and router of enemies,
> Prince of wide fame, they drew up their ranks.
>
> There is a fine fortress on the ninth wave.
> Finely its populace take their ease.
> They do not make merry with taunts and sneers,
> It is not their custom to be hard,
> Nor shall I traduce their welcome -

Better a slave in Dyfed than yeoman in Deudraeth!*
Their throng of free men, keeping a feast,
Would include, two by two, the best men alive!
There is a fine fortress of revel and tumult
A multitude makes and crying of birds..
Gay was that company met at the Calends
Round a generous lord, splendid and brave.
Before he had gone to the oaken church
From a bowl of glass gave me mead and wine.

There is a fine fortress on the foreshore,
Finely to each is given his share.
I know at Tenby - pure white the seagull -
Companions of Bleiddudd, lord of the court.
The night of the Calends it was my custom
To lie by my king, brilliant in war,
With a cloak coloured purple, having such cheer
I were the tongue to the poets of Britain!

There is a fine fortress resounds with song,
Where every concession I wished for was mine -
I say nothing of rights! I kept good order:
Whoever knows otherwise deserves no feast-gift!
The writings of Britain were my chief care
Where the loud waves broke in tumult.
Let it long remain, that cell I visited!

There is a fine fortress on the height,
Its feasting lavish, its revelry loud.
Lovely about it, that camp of heroes,
Is the wandering spray, long are its wings.
Hoarse sea-birds haunt the crest of the crag.
Let all anger be banished over the hills!
I wish for Bleiddudd the best bliss that may be -
Let these words of remembrance be weighed at his wake!

*In Merionethshire, North Wales.

> translated from the Welsh by Anthony Conran.

16

The Harbour

The harbour is the focal point of Tenby. It is sheltered by Castle Hill, which has the white Albert Memorial on its summit. Coloured cottages lead down Pier Hill to The Albion, Laston House, the quay and landing steps. The harbour is full of activity from fishing-boats, yachts, cruising boats, and the boats forming the Caldey "Pool", which sail across to the island during the summer months. In the past, the harbour was so full of craft that it was possible to walk across it by stepping from boat to boat, and some idea of the number of these craft can be gained from Charles Norris' etchings in the Museum on Castle Hill.

St. Julian's Chapel, the Seamen's Church, today stands on a small stone quay below the hill leading to the harbour beach, and was opened in 1878. The original Chapel used to stand on the old pier head, which ran out from the rocks below Castle Square for about 150 yards. This pier, or jetty, did not follow a straight line, but curved towards the south side of the harbour, and the Chapel stood about fifteen yards from the almost circular pier-head. The burgesses of Tenby received grants from Edward III in 1328 to help them to construct this quay and, until the reign of Charles II, Tenby was the only South Wales town possessing a pier.

The importance of the harbour is shown by the fact that once the salary of the Harbour Master, who was called the Quay Warden, was £35 per annum, which was the same amount as that of the Town Clerk, but the latter also included a Stationery allowance!

Services used to be performed regularly in St. Julian's Chapel and, before the fishermen set out to sea, prayers were offered up for their safety and successful fishing. The minister was paid a tithe of one halfpenny for each man and one penny for each boat.

Towards the end of the 18th century, the services in the chapel were discontinued and the payment of tithes came to an end. There are stories of past disputes between the Rector and the fishermen, in which the cry was "no tithes, no fish".

The fishermen's destination was usually Willes' Mark, a fishing-ground situated between Caldey, Lundy, and Worm's Head, Gower, which can be seen directly across Carmarthen Bay from Tenby. This ground swarmed with millwell, ling, congers, breams, gernets and, according to an ancient document "fowls do flock about it very much in the summer". Directions to find Willes' Mark were complicated. Charles Norris, the 19th century artist, quotes from a Corporation document in his "Etchings of Tenby":

"And there was a South coast man came to John Rogers, Major of Tenby, 1626, and divers of the Aldermen of Tenby, that he came by chance on a Rock about halfway betwixt Lundy and Caldy in a calm, and let fall his anchor and finding himself on a rock he sounded and found about eighteen fathoms of water on it. And he cast out fishing lines, within two hours or thereabouts, he took as much fish as he sold in Tenby the next day by retale that he made twenty Nobles of it. And had fish to serve his kettle till he went home to the South coast again".

Another description, reprinted from the "Pembroke County Guardian" says that "this rock at low water lies in some places not above seven or eight fathoms under water; it is supposed to be larger than Caldey Island; it lies in the centre of a triangle, whose angles are Wormshead Point, Caldey Island and Lundy." The old fishermen of Tenby found the mark under sailing directions which "brought the windmill of Tenby over the Chapel of Caldey 'top for top'". The two windmills standing on high ground to the north of Tenby were a well-known landmark.

Lewis Morris, in his Survey, said that the Tenby fishermen lost this fishery by growing rich and indolent. Edward Laws gives an account of the efforts of the Mayor, John Rogers, to recover it. This was some thrity years before John Ray, the scholar and naturalist, visited the Tenby area in 1662.

However, there is an old tradition that Tenby's prosperity only declined after the visit of a deaf and dumb beggar to the town. A few years before this happened, some pirates who had anchored in Caldey Roads had sent a spy ashore, who was caught. When this spy was examined by the Mayor, he had pretended to be deaf and dumb, but had been proved guilty of spying, and was hanged by the local authority on Garrowtree Hill, where gallows remained until 1850.

When this second deaf and dumb beggar appeared, the suspicious Mayor offered a reward to anyone who would flog him. A man called "Leekie Porridge" accepted the offer and, seizing the beggar, carried him to the Norton end of the town. The poor mute fell upon his knees and begged for mercy, but the sentence was carried out. He was so badly injured that he only managed, with considerable difficulty, to climb up the "Slippery Back", now the road at the side of the Cemetery, to a place above the Chapel. Here he fell on his knees and stretched out his hands towards Tenby, cursing the town and its inhabitants.

At once, says the legend, the codfish all left Willes' Mark and the prosperity of the town ceased until the last man who had sanctioned the cruel outrage had died. After this, it is said, the town began to regain its prosperity.

Superstition said that the man who flogged the beggar, and his children after him, were unable to grow beards for four generations. It is also said that the Mayor's child remained speechless all its life and that his wife died as an indirect result of the curse.

Tenby's trade was described in the "Cambrian Traveller's Guide", (second edition 1813) as follows:-

"The trade of Tenby consists of coal and culm and the oyster and trawle fisheries. The first is carried on by vessels of from 30 to 150 tons burthen, which convey coal and culm to various places in the Bristol, Irish and British Channels. They take in their cargoes chiefly at Saundersfoot at three miles distant. In the year 1803, there was cleared out at the Custom House 539 vessels, their cargoes amounting to about 45,000 tons. The oyster fishery yields a supply of from 30 to 40 thousand in a day. They are chiefly shipped for Liverpool and Bristol; others are pickled and sent in jars to London and other places."

Caldey oysters were large and used to be exported widely. One item from the Order Book, dated October 17th 1780, states:

"It having been made appear to the Mayor and Common Council of the Borough that many avaricious persons have in a great measure destroyed the oyster fishery on Caldy bed, owing to their taking oysters of too small a size for Pickling. We, the Mayor and Council, do unanimously agree that if in future any dredging-boat shall presume in taking any small oysters on the said bed, without throwing the same overboard (excepting a quarter of a hundred each man) shall be fined ....."

In spite of this, the oyster beds were over-dredged and the industry came to an end. Caldey oysters were said to be of such a size that one of them would make a meal for two people!

Brixham trawlers carried on a considerable fishing-trade until the early twentieth century. Mackerel in Tenby were so plentiful that they were ten a penny, and the quantity unsold was used as manure. 30 oysters from Caldey beds were 2d, 12 whitings 1d, in 1837. Occasionally a rare fish turned up, such as an angel fish or a twelve foot shark, the latter being pulled ashore in a dying condition on the south beach. A huge sun-fish was also captured. The industry later moved to Milford Haven, where it is today in severe decline.

The curtain wall from Whitesand Gate to the old Inner Harbour Gate, drawn by Charles Norris, who leaves us invaluable records of old buildings of Tenby, was six feet at the highest point. Inside this wall, the fishermen used to collect when bad weather prevented them from going to sea. For this reason, it was known as Penniless Cove.

At Christmas time, the fishermen dressed up one of their number, whom they called "The Lord Mayor of Penniless Cove", with evergreens, flowers and ribbons, and put a mask over his face. This man was seated on a chair with flags flying and a couple of violins being played before him. The procession stopped in front of every house, and the "Lord Mayor" addressed the occupants wishing them a "Merry Christmas and a Happy New Year". If these good wishes resulted in money being given to the Lord Mayor, his followers would give three cheers, the masquer would himself return thanks, and the crowd would again give "three times three" hip hip hurrah's!

The Tenby Improvement Act of 1838, now in Tenby Museum, quotes the following Harbour dues for all vessels coming "within the Part of the Bay lying between the said Borough (Tenby) and a straight line drawn between a Rock called the Skurr Rock, at the Point of the Saint Catherine Rock, and the Northern Extremity of the Sea Boundary of the said Borough", this providing that no "Rate, Toll, or Duty shall be levied upon any Ship, Steam Packet, Boat, Lighter, Barge or other Vessel, unless the same shall come within the Harbour ...or shall make use of any Pier, Slip or Landing Place therein ..."

> For all Trading Vessels (except Fishing Smacks), any Sum not exceeding Three-pence per Ton Register:
> For every Vessel or Boat which shall be laid up in ordinary for the Winter, per Ton Sixpence, and for any other Time, not exceeding Three Months, per Ton Three-pence:
> For all Pleasure Boats or Yachts, per Ton Two-pence, or, at the Option of the Owner or Master, per Ton yearly or for a less Period Sixpence:
> For all Fishing Vessels, per Ton Two-pence, or, at the Option of the Master or Owner, yearly or for a less Period Two Pounds for every such Vessel:

For all Dredging Boats, per Annum or for any less Period Five Shillings:

All Ships Boats, and Boats bona fide and solely used for pitching or piloting Vessels, to be exempt.

The name "Scur", "Skurr" or "Sker", the rock beyond St. Catherine's Point, probably stems from the Norse "Skera", which is "Ploughshare". Goscar Rock on the North Beach was thought by Charles Norris to be "God's Plough".

St. Julien's Chapel

17

Buildings of Tenby

A local expression which is occasionally used by some of the older people in Tenby today, refers to the "Twelve Steps": "If you're not careful, you'll be going down the twelve steps!" This is said to refer to the magistrates court and gaol, where the Charity Trustees now meet, and there is a plaque on the wall below the archway to this effect. The entrance to the court was from the churchyard, in the rear of the premises, which has a flight of twelve steps and below these was the gaol.

If you had been found guilty of an offence and taken down these steps to prison, you might have know the four Tenby policemen referred to in a rhyme composed by a Tenbyite. In 1877, a Cardiff policeman, William Henry Hodges, was appointed Superintendent. Another appointment followed, that of James Carr, an ex-soldier, stockily built, with his hair parted down the middle. He was promptly named "Jack of Clubs" by the local people. He was well-read, intelligent and a tactful and friendly man. Another constable was apparently a local man named Beynon. The last recruit was a young man from Llangadock, Richard James Pulker, of smart appearance, who commanded many admiring glances. The rhyme ran:

"Here comes Carr all in full sail,
Then comes Beynon under his tail,
Then comes Pulker, smiling so sweet,
Then comes Hodges, and spoils the whole fleet!"

The so-called "Flemish chimneys" are a noticeable part of the local architecture in Tenby. These massive chimneys, some round, some angular, stand on a round or square base and are found on old buildings, "from the labourer's cottage to the baronial hall and the episcopal palace". None of them is earlier than the fourteenth century.

Nothing resembles them in the Low Countries. Neither George Owen nor Fenton mentioned them, but Charles Norris said he had seen them at Coniston Hall in Cumberland, on the banks of Coniston Lake. This was a family mansion belonging to the Le Flemings. He also says:-

"The people, by whom these edifices were erected, originally came over to the assistance of William the Conqueror, under their leader Sir Michael Le Fleming",

but Edward Laws suggests:

"The late Mr. Norris, I rather expect, evolved the Flemish chimney out of his own inner consciousness"!

Today Charles Norris is thought to be the originator of their myth.

A narrow flight of steps leads up to the entrance of many Flemish houses, with a low Gothic porch above to give protection to the inhabitants. Numerous corbels are a feature, as ornaments "of no apparent usefulness".

Woollen manufacture in Tenby was possibly established by the Flemings, but to what extent is not known. There is a tradition believed in by Tenby people that they had two woollen factories, one on Castle Hill and another in Chimney Park. The tower on Castle Hill is said to be the oldest building in Tenby, and from it can be seen the Woolhouse Rocks, a reef two miles south-east of the shore and so-called because they resembled newly carded wool. The discontinuance of weaving was said to be due to an epidemic, and Charles Norris believed that the weavers fled from Tenby to Devonshire because of it.

Windmills were introduced into Western Europe by the Crusaders returning from the east. Tenby had at least three almost three centuries later, but they were so old as to be "utterly decayed". A fourth windmill was later erected near the town.

In the grounds of "Rosemount" near Heywood Lane, this windmill stood close to the site of the Hospital of St. Mary Magdalene in the Maudlins. The mill was decayed in the time of Queen Elizabeth, and it does not appear to have been used again after this date.

St. Mary's, the parish Church of Tenby, was one of the largest medieval churches in Wales. When Gerald the Welshman (Giraldus Cambrensis) became first Rector in 1210, he complained that he had not received the tithe due to him from the fishing trade, Tenby being at that time well-known for its productive fisheries.

Visitors to Tenby in 1868 said that the Church had "A fine square tower, in which there are a set of six bells, and on east and west sides a public clock". The old clock had rude limestone weights. On one of the bells, the tenor bell, the following inscription could be seen:
"I to the church the living call,
And to the grave doth summon all".

The story of a silver-lined bell is told by Philip H. Gosse, the nineteenthcentury marine biologist, who wrote "laboured and scientific volumes". On his way to Hean Castle, near Saundersfoot, he was told by his coachman:

"Do you see that ruined mansion, Sir, to the right among the trees, all covered with ivy? That is Scotsborough, the ancient seat of the famous Ap Rhys. The house is half a mile from Tenby and he could not always hear the Church-bell; so he lined the bell with silver at his own expense, that he might hear when to go to Church. The bell now hangs outside the tower at Tenby, and anybody can see it is lined with silver".

Gosse asked the name of these two ruins and was told that they were Trefloyne and Scotsborough.

"But what caused the ruin of these two fine houses?"

The coachman replied:

"Oh, Sir, that is more than I can tell. There's many fine mansions, in all parts of Wales that now lie in ruins under the green ivy; but I have heard say that the two families that inhabited Trefloyne and Scotsborough lived by wrecking. They put false lights on the windmill at the end of the South Cliffs, just over the cavern where they used to store their plunder. This went on well enough for a time; but it was the end of the families, for the only son of one family and the only daughter of the other, were coming home from abroad, and were wrecked through the false lights, and what is strange, the ship went ashore on the sands just opposite the mouth of the cave".

The Ritec marsh was once a creek and boats were able to sail right up to Scotsborough, passing Hoyle's Mouth cave. Scotsborough stands two miles to the west of Tenby and was garrisoned for King Charles in the Civil Wars.

St. Mary's Church steeple, dominating the skyline, is a landmark for those at sea, as well as on land. The people of Tenby were always fond of bell-ringing, and used to ring the bells on every occasion, births, marriages, deaths, and also to call people to Church, as they still do today.

According to legend, one Sunday afternon one of the ringers saw a tune marked out in numbers on the wall, and began to ring it. The Rector, who was just coming to church, listened and was very surprised to hear the well-known popular tune called "Bob and Joan" ringing from the church bells! At once, a stop was put to Sunday chiming.

Wirt Sikes, who was United States Consul for Wales, published his "British Goblins" in 1880. Speaking of Tenby, he says:-

"At Tenby, when the High Sheriff's son was married to the Rector of Tenby's daughter in 1877, garlands of flowers were hung across the High Street, bearing pleasant mottoes, while flags and banners fluttered from house-tops in all directions. Children strewed flowers in the bride's path as she came out of church, while the bells in the steeple chimed a merry peal, and a park of miniature artillery boomed from the pier-head".

Tenby bells were also rung out to welcome back William Richards, the Mayor, who was injured in a duel fought on April 1st 1839 with Henry Mannix of Sion House, later Woofferton Grange.

There had been a dispute over a plot of land, which the Mayor sought to recover for the Council. A protest over its enclosure was made in a letter from Charles Norris, who was referred to by Richards as "that madman"! Richards, who was injured by a shot which lodged near his spine, was attended by three surgeons and spent some weeks at Clifton recovering from his injury. The duel took place near the old Causeway Mill at the foot of Gumfreston Hill, and the news of it was given by Mr. George Hughes, who witnessed it and rode to the Anchor Inn (the Coburg Hotel) with an account of Richard's injury.

Among the many tombs, monuments and tablets in the Church, which are fully documented elsewhere, there is a mutilated statue of a kneeling figure. This monument is in memory of William Risam, who died in 1633, and his family provided mayors and bailiffs for Tenby for several generations. It is said that a Cromwellian trooper thought the figure was a living target and aimed his musket at the statue.

When the Church roof was being repaired in 1842, a cannon-ball, probably fired during the siege of Tenby by Cromwell's troops, was found in one of the beams. The west window in the north aisle of the Church was utterly destroyed during the Civil Wars. William Risam left a bequest to the town:-

> Two hundred pounds
> and fifty more
> he gave this towne
> to help the poore
>
> The use of one on clothe
> And coles bestowe
> For twelve decreped meane
> and low

>   let fifty pounds to five
>   be yearely lent
>   the others use on burgess
>   sonnes be spent

Perhaps the most curious of tablets is that in remembrance of Peggy Davies, who was "Bathing woman forty-two years to the ladies who visited Tenby". She was noted for "her good humour, her respectful attention and gratitude which made her Employers friends. On the 29th September 1809 in the water she was seized with apoplexy and expired aged 82".

Ancient Building adjoining White's House

18

The Escape of Henry VII From Tenby

In the year 1457, when Henry VII was born in Pembroke Castle, the people of Tenby rebuilt the walls of their town. When these walls were further strengthened against the threat of the Spanish Armada, Tenby became one of the principal fortresses in South Wales.

Edward IV recovered his throne in 1471, and it was no longer safe for Henry (of Richmond), grandson of Owen Tudor, to remain in Wales. His uncle Jasper took him across the sea, meaning to convey him to France. The wind, however, compelled them to land in Brittany where they found asylum with Duke Francis II.

The only historical account of this escape is given in "Anglicae Historiae", Libri XXVI, a chronicle written by Polydore Vergil, a native of Urbino, who came to England in 1502. This states that they came to Tenby from Pembroke and sailed to Brittany. A crop of highly-coloured legends have arisen from this event, based upon a misinterpretation of George Owen's version of the story, written in about 1575. It is said that the fugitives were hospitably received by the Mayor of Tenby, John White, a wealthy merchant, who hid them in the wine cellars under his house, two of which were connected by a secret passage. He was further said to have sent them on a small vessel of his own to France, and to have been rewarded, when Henry VII came to the throne, by a lease given to him of all the King's lands about Tenby.

The Crown Lands were not leased to Mr. White "auncestor to Mr. Harrye White of Henllan, nowe lyveinge, then Mayor of Tenby for his good service" as Owen states, but they were granted to John White by Richard III, while the Earl of Richmond was still in retreat in Brittany. In this grant, John White was obliged to render annually a Red Rose to the King, who represented the White Rose of York. The grant is dated 12th February 1484.

White's House used to be on the site of the present Boots the Chemists, and the cellars still exist under the High Street, a little to the North of the Church gate.

The French Invasion and Tenby's Alarm

When the French landed at Fishguard on the 22nd February 1797, the mistaken news reached Tenby that they had landed at Freshwater Bay, just beyond Manorbier. The townspeople were very alarmed and the Volunteers were called out. Guns were put into working order, while a general arming took place. Sentinels were posted and a gallant defence was prepared.

Quite shortly afterwards, the correct place of landing was confirmed and a messenger was sent to Fishguard to learn the true facts.

On Friday night the 25th, in thick darkness in Tenby, the sentinel was pacing his solitary way at the north entrance to the town. He suddenly heard the sound of horses' feet approaching quickly. Very much afraid, he heard the horse coming nearer, until he saw what appeared to be one of the enemy's cavalry.

"Who goes there? he demanded.

The horseman recognised the sentinel's voice as that of his man-servant, and wishing to test his courage, paid no attention to the challenge but pressed on. The sentinel began to retire up the Norton shouting:

"Who goes there?"

After a time, the gentleman on horseback burst out laughing and the sentinel, realising the situation, cried out:

"Ah! master it is lucky you spoke, else in another moment you'd have been a dead man!"

This proof of the sentinel's courage was a standing joke against him as long as he lived!

The following day, the messenger sent to Fishguard from Tenby returned with ribbons in his hat and coat, his horse's head decked out, bringing news of the French surrender. Inhabitants soon went to dig up their hidden treasures, buried for safety, "when much to the surprise of some, they had disappeared"!

The Old Gun Fort

The old Gun Fort on the South Cliff is now converted into the Paragon Gardens. Nine eighteen-pounder guns used to be in position there, where the Sea Fencibles, raised at the time of Buonaparte's threatened invasion, met each week for gun exercise.

In about 1813, this gun fort was the scene of a midnight adventure. A young lady of Tenby, "who was accompanied by three gentlemen visitors", carried out a practical joke. They loaded the guns by lantern light and fired them in quick succession. The culprits then ran off and the inhabitants of Tenby rushed in alarm from their beds. The three involved in the incident escaped undiscovered from Tenby the next morning, while "the lady kept her secret".

To the east of Gunfort was a deep chine, which ran from the shore continuing across St. Julian's Street. This was known as Brechmaenchine, or the Chine of the Spotted Stone, possibly because the cliff was speckled with fossil oyster-shells. A flight of rough steps running down to the shore was probably connected with a sallyport in the wall. These steps are still known to older local people as "Break Man's Shins".

Tower near South Gate

19

Visitors and Benefactors

Tenby had many visitors, who left accounts of their impressions and experiences, as they travelled through Pembrokeshire.

John Leland, in the sixteenth century, said that the town had the only existing pier in Wales.

George Owen wrote his "History of the County of Pembrokeshire" in 1590. He was described as "a learned and ingenious person" and his manuscript account of the change of level in the county is as follows:-

"About twelve or thirteen years since, it happen'd that the sea-sands at Newgal (Newgale), which are cover'd every tide, were by some extraordinary violence of the waves so wash'd off, that there appear'd stocks of trees, doubtless in their native place; for they retain'd manifest signs of the strokes of the axe, at the falling of them. The sands being wash'd off, in the winter these buts remain'd to be seen all the summer following but the next year the same were cover'd again with the sands.

"Moreover, I have been told by the neighbours of Coed Traeth near Tenby, that the like hath been seen also upon those sands.

"Similar remains have also been noticed on the opposite (Somersetshire) coast".

Richard Mason says in "Tales and Traditions of Tenby":

"An extensive tract of country, covering the site of the Bristol Channel, part of St. George's Channel, and the whole of Cardigan Bay sunk beneath the level of the sea.

but he comments:

"Certain changes have taken place in the neighbourhood of Tenby occasioned by the elevation of a portion of this district."

In the latter half of 1657, George Fox, the Quaker, visited Tenby. He was well received and a Justice of the Peace asked him to stay at his house. The Mayor and Mayoress attended his meeting. One John ap John, a fervent Quaker, left the Meeting-house and strolled into the Parish Church, where he was arrested by order of the Governor.

When Fox heard this, he sought out the Governor and asked why his friend was cast into prison. The Governor answered "for standing with his hat on in the Parish Church"! A long dialogue took place and John ap John was released, the Governor asking Fox to dinner. They went back afterwards to the magistrate's house and he, the Mayor, their wives and others went with the Quakers to the waterside (the Ritec) about half a mile from the town when prayers were said (Archaeologia Cambrensis 1898 p.70) In 1763, Wesley rode from Laugharne to Tenby in rain and reached Tenby at about 11 a.m. "The rain then ceased and I preached at the Cross (in Market Street) to a congregation gathered from many miles around. The sun broke out several times and shone hot in my face, but never for two minutes together".

Edward Laws, in "A Gentleman's Tour through Monmouthshire and Wales in the months of June and July 1774" said of Pembrokeshire:

"There are few inclosures, but no common feed, every proprietor having private right to the pasture of his own ground only, and no other; this circumstance is attended with much inconvenience both to the owner of lands and to the traveller. For there being no common sheep herd, all the horses, sheep and even poultry, are staked at the end of a line to the ground, in order to prevent mutual trespass; the consequence being that the ropes frequently cross the high road and entangle the horse's feet of the unwary traveller".

Edward Laws' "History of Little England Beyond Wales" was published in 1888 by F. B. Mason at the Observer Office, and also in London.

In the eighteenth century, J. W. M. Turner, the artist, came to the area. Walter Savage Landor, Woodward, Matthews and Mrs. Morgan Skrine were all travellers who left notes on what they had seen.

Lord Nelson, as Admiral of the Fleet, visited Tenby with Sir William and Lady Hamilton in 1802. They dined at Amroth and then visited Frog Street, Tenby, for a performance of "The Mock Doctor" at the Blue Ball Inn. There was a strolling player in the town, a Mr. Gore, who wrote of the public attention given to the party in Tenby. Emma was at this time caricatured savagely for her enormous size, loud vulgar laugh and large feet. She was, for this outing, dressed in a "white cotton Indian dress, red morocco waistband fastened with a diamond buckle, red morocco slippers and diamond buckles. Nelson devoted to her the greater part of the evening."

The Alfred Morrison collection of letters in the North Library of the British Museum includes a sheet of accounts in Nelson's handwriting, which is dated between 20th July and 21st September 1802. Apparently, Nelson and Sir William Hamilton agreed to share expenses for a tour to Milford and Nelson kept the accounts:

Bill at Tenby	£ 8	7	6
Servants		7	6
Horses as by bill from Narberth, Stackpole, Pembroke, Tenby and St. Clears	14	4	4
Drivers	1	8	0

At the end of the eighteenth century, many alterations took place to the town of Tenby. The Order Book of Tenby Corporation states:

"Borough of Tenby - Ordered that a lease of the Chapel on the Pier (being Quay land) be granted to John Jones, B. of Physics, of the Town and County of Haverfordwest, for the sole purpose of constructing baths and other contrivances, for the term of three lives, viz:- the Princess Sophia, the Princess Octavius and Alfred, the three youngest children of his present Majesty, for the yearly rent of one shilling per annum to commence this thirteenth day of November 1781."

As the Chapel was very small, it is most likely that the "contrivances" were simply a heating apparatus erected for a hot salt water bath for his patients. Although the Chapel had degenerated into a blacksmith's forge in 1812, according to Charles Norris, it was in use as a bathing-house up to 1805, the year in which Sir William Paxton's more pretentious establishment was commenced.

Sir William Paxton, Knight, of Middleton Hall, Carms, took up residence in the town in 1805. Edward Laws states that he bought two properties, one originally belonging to the White family, and the other to Sir Roger Lort, and known as the Stackpole Estate. Paxton's House is now Tenby House, on the site of the Globe Hotel. In the same year, the following entry appears in the Order book:

"Whereas Sir William Paxton, of Middleton Hall in the County of Carmarthen, Knight, has proposed for the prosperity of this ancient Borough to build a bathing house on premises leased to him this day by the Corporation, it is ordered that the Freedom of this Corporation be presented to him as a token of respect and gratitude, and he is hereby ordered by the Mayor and Common Council to be admitted a Burgess of this Borough, this seventeenth day of October 1805".

No sooner were the new Baths built at the foot of Castle Hill, than they were burnt down. Sir William rebuilt them and, until his death in 1824, continued to heap benefits upon the town. The architect for the baths was Mr. Cockerell. Fenton says:

"Large reservoirs containing many thousand tons, were so contrived as to change their water every tide, and furnish enough to feed all the different baths in the intervals".

Today you can see the motto of the town of Tenby above the door of Laston House, the site of the baths, which in translation from the Greek, is "The sea washes away all the ills of men", a quotation from Euripides (Iphigenia In Tauris, line 1,193).

Paxton also presented the ruins of White's House to the Corporation, to be removed in order to improve the High Street, and he built the arches on which Bridge Street stands. He established a theatre and, when this failed, bought the building so that his associates could not be out of pocket. His death was a bitter blow to Tenby. For twenty years, he had spent large sums of money on improvements to the town.

With the arrival of the Railway in 1863, the prosperity of the town increased. The lower portion of the town was almost rebuilt and a quarter sprung up between the station and the sea. Improved transport brought new visitors to Tenby. Gosse wrote in 1856 that the coaches from Narberth to Tenby were called Coburg and White Lion. They were four-in-hand, and the whole population of villages turned out to watch the Great Exhibition of the day, the coaches passing by! This journey ended with a cup of tea at the Coburg for passengers on the coach of that name.

One well-known traveller was the Victorian Mrs. S. C. Hall. Born in Dublin, she published more than fifty books, entertained spiritualists and street musicians and helped to found the Hospital for Consumptives at Brompton, and also the Home for Decayed Gentlewomen. Her account of her travels with her husband was published by Richard Mason at Tenby. It is undated and has many illustrations in black and white, with old engravings of the Tenby area. She gives a spirited account of the confusion caused by the arrival of the pirate, Paul Jones, at Tenby.

In 1897, the Victoria Pier was built, and it was finished in 1899 with some private financial aid. This deep-water Pier was proposed because according to the Prospectus:

"The Steamboat Service from Bristol and other ports has been carried on for many years under great disadvantage and inconvenience, as there is only sufficient depth of water for a short space of time at high tide to enable these vessels to come alongside the present harbour jetty, and passengers have to be landed in small boats, and the vessel will remain till the following tide in order to discharge her cargo. It may therefore be reasonably anticipated that a greater passenger and goods traffic must result with such perfect accommodation as the Company's Pier will afford".

It was said that "landing at Tenby was "very disagreeable to Ladies".

The maintenance of this pier was not carried out sufficiently to keep it in good order, and it had to be destroyed after estimates for repairs proved too expensive. The old steps and the light standards can be seen today above the rocks where the old pier stood, just to the right of the present Lifeboat Slip on Castle Hill.

The Victoria Pier

20

Caldey Island and St. Margaret's

Thirteen centuries ago, Caldey was joined to the mainland, but today it is an island one and a half miles south-south-east of Tenby. The south-westerly side of the island is old red sandstone, while the Tenby side is mountain limestone. At the junction of these two types of rock, rich fossil remains have been found, and a magnificent spring breaks out, which waters the whole island and fills a large fishpond. This spring is said to be supplied by the mainland and to pass under the sea in this water-bearing strata.

St. Piro, who became Abbot of Caldey, lived as a hermit on the island in the sixth century. The monastery began as a small group of wattle huts erected round a chapel. The island's Welsh name is Ynys Pŷr, or Piro's island.

During Lent on a dark night, St. Piro was walking in the grounds of the Monastery and being, according to the legend rather drunk, he fell into a deep pit. He was dragged out of it, but died as a result of his injuries. The next morning, St. Samson, who had been brought up, instructed and ordained at Llantwit Major, was elected unanimously as the new Abbott. Samson's father, mother and his whole family of brothers, except for one sister, all became monks or nuns, establishing many monasteries and convents in Pembrokeshire.

On one of his journeys to Caldey with his father and uncle, St. Samson met a serpent on the path. St. Samson had just restored his father to health and was known for his magical healing powers. The legend says that he confined the snake with the mystic sign of an impassable circle and killed it with one word. The party was able to continue their journey to Caldey over the rocks on foot.

Charles Norris states in his "Account of Tenby":
"There used to be three religious houses upon Caldey, one near the beach on the north side, another on the highest point of the land above the south cliff, and a third near to the centre of the island. The present one, part of which is of great antiquity, with a stone spire, was a cell dependant on the Abbey of St. Dogmaels".

The remains of fourteenth-century buildings join the Priory, which has its stone spire out of perpendicular and all its tower apartments vaulted. It is supposed to have been founded by Robert, son of Martin de Turribus (Martin of Tours). Behind these buildings is the farm with fruit trees and gardens, the prolific spring being under an enclosed building.

Fenton says: "In the ruins of the Priory, a gravestone was dug up, inscribed with the name of Cadwgan". He believed it to commemorate one of the early priors of Caldey. This stone had served the office of lintel to a window, and Fenton found it in Mr. Kynaston's garden. The exact spot is said to have been in front of the blacksmith's shop, which once stood east of the well. There are many references to this stone, which has one Latin and one Ogham inscription, dated between the sixth and eighth centuries.

According to an old story, Caldey was once smaller than it is today. The monastery was so near to the sea that it was sometimes flooded. St. Illtud prayed that the island might be enlarged, and it then rose sufficiently far out of the sea to prevent flooding in the future. This could also refer to the change of level in the area. It is said that, at this time, the young St. David was a pupil at St. Illtud's school.

A black robed monk, over six feet tall, is said to wander round the old Priory, and is thought to be the ghost of a madman. The legend says that a monk brought treasure of gold plate and altar vessels to Caldey from Glastonbury for safety in the time of Henry VIII. But when these valuable articles were no longer safe on the island, he concealed these items and then bricked himself in with them, suffocating to death. Although a "luninous glow" is supposed to indicate the burial plot of hidden treasure, according to the inhabitants of Caldey, the treasure has not yet been discovered.

Edward Laws, who said the sanctity of the island stretched into prehistoric days, also discovered that "in the north-western corner, near St. Margaret's Island, is a well-defined fragment of a raised beach. From the old to the recent beach is a twelve foot drop." An old road could be distinguished in the turf.

Mr. and Mrs. S. C. Hall travelled over to Caldey on their tour of the area and said:

"The substantial manor house faces Penally and Tenby and has a lawn in front with a flagstaff, a plantation beside the lawn, and two flower gardens; the gold-fish are left in a small open pond throughout the winter, because of the mild climate."

One hundred years ago, a small carved alabaster receptacle, dating from the fourteenth century, was found lying hidden in a rock crevice. It had been there since the dissolution of the Benedictine Priory in 1536.

The parish Church on the island is dedicated to St. David, and was at one time just above the high water mark. It is said that it was originally dedicated to St. Mary-on-the-Seashore for this reason. The monks and local inhabitants are buried in the churchyard in sandy soil under pine trees. The monks' graves are marked with simple wooden crosses, their heads are covered but they have no coffins. Behind the wall of the Churchyard are the Monastery grounds.

Caldey Island has been occupied or visited regularly over the centuries by Neolithic men, travellers, pirates and geologists. Nanna's Cave, high up on the cliff-face has produced important Romano-British relics.

Two caves were also discovered at Eel Point, one of these sheltering human inhabitants in the past. Fossil remains of elephant, hyena and deer were also found. Most of these remains were discovered over a hundred years ago by the Reverend Gilbert N. Smith (1796 - 1877) of Gumfreston, and his collection is the foundation of the Tenby Museum. He described the cave in a paper which he sent to Mrs. F. Allen of Cresselly, who was related to Charles Darwin, then Secretary of the Geological Society of London. She replied on August 19th: "I forwarded your paper to Mr. Charles Darwin; it found him unfortunately very ill in bed, but it has excited his interest very much and he wrote down a list of questions which he would be obliged to you to answer". Darwin wanted to secure precise information on several points, in order to read the paper to the Geological Society but, for an unknown reason Smith did not return the questions to him.

Smith's peculiarities used to bring in visitors to Tenby. One occasion, while preaching at Gumfreston, he divided his hearers into three: first those who feared God; secondly those who feared men; and thirdly those who feared the devil. After describing the first, he said:

"The second are a good-natured set of fellows, who will drink with anyone and who will say to any chance acquaintance: 'Here is a shilling for you (holding one in his hand); the third are those profane men who have driven here from Tenby".

He once called out from the pulpit: "I won't preach till all the Tenby people are out of the Church"!

When speaking on his favourite subject, the wonders of creation, he quoted from his own published lecture. Catching sight of the publisher in Church, he said:

"I see my friend Mr. Mason from Tenby here. You can buy the lecture from him for a shilling; it is cheap at the price."

Referring to Herodias dancing before Herod, he said:

"They tell me there is dancing going on at Tenby that would please Herod a good deal more than it would either me or John the Baptist"!

There have recently been excavations on the island by Brother James, a keen archaeologist who, several years ago, made an exciting find of two skulls in Nanna's Cave, where there is a pit chamber. His find has proved that Caldey was once joined to the mainland thirteen centuries ago. In 1910, monks cutting a pathway through an ancient furze brake on the northern cliff, discovered certain dykes cut in the live rock.

John Ray, in "A Naturalist's Tour in Pembrokeshire in 1662" said he had "passed over Caldey Isle, of which Mr. Williams is owner". He noted that the rarer plants growing included "the tree-mallow, the golden Samphire, vernal squill, sea-spleenwort and a kind of tithymalus".

Mr. and Mrs. S. C. Hall found that fern used to be gathered by the inhabitants and stacked for fuel and thatching. As it grew abundantly, "it also supplied the public oven, which was attended to for a week at a time by each of the housewives in turn".

Caldey gorse is world-famous. It was once crushed and fed to cattle, and the stalks used for heating bread ovens. The blossom was used for a golden wine, called by Augustus John, the artist, "Gorse Champagne". Caldey found the process for extracting oil from gorse flowers to make perfume, and they have the only perfumery in the world which uses this process. Although farming is carried on, transport to the mainland presents problems in the winter, and the island is not large enough for this to be commercially profitable. Prize pigs used to be raised, and also pountry, but both these enterprises have been abandoned.

Local boatmen say that every flower mentioned in Shakespeare grows on Caldey. There is, according to them, one species of primula which will only grow in its true colour on this island. If it is moved, it changes its hue.

Sixty years ago, the return fare from Tenby to Caldey on the S.S. Firefly was two shillings. Passengers who landed from other boats, not belonging to the island community, were charged sixpence each.

Richard Mason, in his "Guide to Tenby" describes his visit to the island in detail, starting with his arrival:

"Leaving the shore and turning to the left of the road leading to the mansion, we passed a slight depression in the ground north east of the cottages, site of an early burying-place, on which some years ago several stone graves (or cistvaens) were discovered. Not far from this was a chapel, in the south wall of which is an early inscribed stone invoking passers-by to pray for the soul of Catuoconus.

"After having a glimpse of Jones' Bay, we came to Little Drinkim Bay, where we descended to the beach. At the bottom of this cliff, we noticed for the first time, traces of iron ore.

"At Great Drinkim Bay, our attention was attracted by beholding numerous small holes burrowed in the sand on the surface of the cliff; they were the cells of a species of bee (anthophora retusa). Sand remarkably of a fine brown. We saw several large veins of hematite iron ore. Close to the veins lay a white clay, a very hard and white sandstone, and a quantity of fine, white sand, suitable for making the clearest species of glass.

"In the same bay we discovered a rock, portions of which were veined with oxide of copper. We followed the strata over the centre of the island to Sandtop Bay, where we again saw the iron ore and white sandstone. A little to the west of Sandtop Bay, we came upon a cliff completely covered with broken pieces of limestone containing crinoidean remains, especially their stems.

"We were, on returning, kindly invited to view the beautiful grounds surrounding the mansion, where we were particularly interested in several ponds, teeming with gold and silver fish. These ponds are plentifully suplied by a never-failing spring of the purest water".

Limestone used to be quarried on Caldey and the houses in Appledore, Devon, are made of Caldey limestone, shipped across to Bristol and Devon. The quarries used mostly women's labour and the workers were paid one shilling a day as wages. Above the quarries stands the watchtower, which was originally used as a look-out for shoals of fish in the bay, but this has now been converted to a Chapel of Rest.

It is said that St. Margaret's Island was once part of Caldey Island, but was separated from it at about 1530 by a great storm. The island is now a bird sanctuary. In Elizabethan times, it was said to bear "good grass for sheep and conies". It had a "store of gulls" and was "in the Queen Majesty's land, parcel of her manor of Manorbier and Penally".

There used to be a small ruined chapel on the island not more than five feet high. One of the owners of Caldey, the Rev. Done Bushell (1897 - 1906) made a ground plan of it, which showed a dormitory and refectory. The size of the island was considerably reduced by limestone quarrying, and the stone-roofed powder house, or stores used for explosives, were still there in 1957.

St. Margaret was the daughter of a heathen priest and was brought up as a Christian by her nurse. She was martyred at Antioch, and many wonderful cures were attributed to her.

On rounding the point of St. Margaret's Gosse says:

"We find ourselves in a little indentation or cave, with lofty perpendicular walls, with wide fissures intervening between columns of solid rock, as straight and clear-edged as if hewn by a statuary, running up to the very summit, which cannot be less than 100 feet high. On the left is a noble perpendicular cavern, the light appears at the farther end, and at high water a boat can pass right through to the other side. The squareness of every feature is remarkable".

George Owen, author of "Elizabethan Pembrokeshire" says: "St. Margaret's should be visited only when the day is fine and the sea calm".

Coins have been found occasionally on the island, especially those of Constantine, and one of Carausius.

John Ray in 1662 said that the island "had gulls, sea-swallows, puits, their nests so thick that a man can scarce walk but he must set his foot upon them".

On the rocks there grows the lavatera arborea, also a type of chrysanthemum. He found small shells on the sand, conchae venera striato' "of which the country people make themselves hat-bands".

Lobster pots are situated around the two island, and Atlantic Grey Seals back on the rocks in sunshine, but vanish under the sea when a boat approaches.

George Owen remarked on the good safe shipping road to the north of Caldey and St. Margaret's. In Elizabethan times, this was "from twelve to six fathoms deep in good ooze, safe for all winds, those of the east points excepted. It may receive between it and the roads of Tenby two hundred ships, as lately certified in a survey, all in safe holding and good anchor hold".

In the winter of 1836, a party of seventeen labourers, including several women, left Caldey Island on Christmas Eve, to spend Christmas Day with relatives and friends in Tenby and its neighbourhood.

The wind blew furiously from the east and the waves rose with such violence that Mr. Kynaston, the owner of the island, strongly urged them to abandon their intention to leave, but the boat left. This account, in Bourne's "Tenby", tells that the boat safely weathered the fury of the wind and waves until nearly abreast of Sker Rock, close to St. Catherine's Island, when she was suddenly upset by a tremendous wave. In a moment, all her passengers were drowned. "The Loss of the Caldey Boat" was remembered for many sad Christmasses to come.

21

Penally and St. Florence

In the "Liber Landavensis", which was compiled in the twelfth century, the Ritec is described as "close to" or "hard by" Penally. At this time, Tenby, Penally, Gumfreston and St. Florence were one great connected lagoon.

Traces of early men, who were fish-eaters, were found here. Near the ruined cottage, named the "Old Quay", just above Hoyle's Mouth cave, and about half-way between the older embankments on the slope of the hill, an old boat was found while draining the land. This was a dug-out hollowed from a single tree.

In prehistoric times, Stackpole had salt-water locks and was a very populous neolithic settlement.

The marshland between Tenby and St. Florence village was reclaimed by several operations. The marsh is noted for its wealth of wild flowers, which formerly included the rare Tenby daffodil. Yellow flags, willow-herb and touch-me-not with hanging blossoms grow in the area.

As late as the nineteenth century, a local resident remembered the time when vessels proceeded nearly a mile over what is now pasture land, as far as Holloway Quarry, where they discharged their cargo at the bottom of Pill Field.

Allen's "Guide to Tenby", published in 1868,m describes the area at that time:

"Vessels were 'laid up' high and dry for the winter, during the last hundred years, beneath the hill near the station, and there is a tradition that, before the old Tenby Pier was built, the primitive harbour was up this estuary. At high water, about seventy years ago, boats used to cruise where the Ritec now flows, a narrow stream. Until the road was raised, over which the Pembroke road now passes the Ritec, the water on spring tides used to cover the road at that place, and there were portions deep enough to be dangerous to passers-by on horseback, while for hours until the tide ebbed, it was impossible for carriages about thirty years since.

"This portion of the road was known as 'Holloway's Water'. A stone bridge with flood-gates was carried across the beach from the Tenby side to the burrows; this is now built over by the embankment of the railway.

"During a dreadful storm, some years ago, the sea burst through the thick stone bridge road, and poured into the flat marsh; part of Saundersfoot's new pier was also washed down at the same time".

Two posts used to stand upon Marsh Road to mark the depth of the spring tide, about one and a half miles from the centre of the town. Mr. Wilson of Hên Castle wrote this account in a letter to Richard Mason of Tenby in 1840, when "Tales and Traditions of Tenby" was being compiled:

"The bridge across the Marsh was being built, the roadway was finished, and the parapet wall partly built. There was a breach in the sea embankment at which the tide came in and, at the springs, came more or less over the bridge. I was riding home one evening when the tide was higher than usual, and I supposed I could go through the water on the bridge at the time, as I had frequently done before. But when about the centre of the bridge, it was so deep that my horse began to feel a buoyancy, got alarmed, sprang over the parapet on the sea side, and I had to swim him, and land near the Holloway Lime-Kiln".

After receiving Mr. Wilson's letter, Richard Mason said that a survey showed the roadway over the centre of Marsh Bridge to be 3 ft. 2 ins. below the average height of the sea wall, and that the roadway was 6 inches higher than the highest tide that had occurred for the last twelve years.

"The road", he said "about 150 yards from the bridge, on the Pembroke side, is however 3 ft. lower, but this does not appear to be the spot alluded to by Mr. Wilson. I can only say that it appears here, as I have so often found in other parts, that the sea is receding, or the land rising".

The sandhills behind Tenby's South Beach are called The Burrows. They were described in the Prospectus of the proposed company, the "Tenby Pier and Promenade Limited" as "covered with rare vegetation, which in the season prove a favourite hunting ground for the Entomologist and the Botanist. Many rare specimens of insect life and wild flowers are found in this locality".

A mile and three-quarters from Tenby, on the Pembroke Road, is Hoyle's Mouth, an ancient limestone stream-cavern. Arthur L. Leach, who was Hon. Curator of Tenby Museum from 1940 - 1957 stated that this cave was once used as a hyena den and was later occupied by Neolithic men. ("Some Prehistoric Remains in the Tenby Museum")

The Reverend Gilbert Smith of Gumfreston spent much time collecting remains here.

Gosse wrote:

"We leave the Pembroke road, and suddenly plunge down into a narrow lane with tall, almost meeting hedges, a perfect wilderness of flowers. There was the crimson Campion, so variable in the size and hue of its blossoms; the coarse blue spikes of bugle; the meadow vetchling, trailing about and throwing its racemes of yellow over the brambles; and the mountain willow-herb, with its white flowers tipped with pink; and the modest, laughing, little forget-me-not and blushing Dog-roses, and sugary honeysuckles in profuse luxuriance. There too was plenty of toadflax, but in leaf only, and only just showing the budding spike, a beautiful plant even so".

He also refers to strawberry, ivy, hart's tongue, spleenworts, while roses trailed over everything.

Thomas Purnell lived in Tenby from 1850 until 1860, when we went to London to become a journalist and dramatic critic. He wrote many of the chapters in Mr. and Mrs. S. C. Hall's book on South Wales and describes the narrow winding path to the cavern, which is "hidden from any one passing below by tangled brushwood and trees of stunted growth".

"Behind the arched entrance the cave contracts to a low and winding passage about 160 feet long, widening here and there into small chambers. Nearly a century ago, Colonel Jervis and Major Pugett broke a way through "The Narrows" where stalactites almost choked the passage. The third and largest chamber, sometimes called "Hoyle's Chamber", beyond which few visitors proceed, is not the last. A very narrow fissure runs in almost vertically for several feet on the left and, on the right, one can crawl through a hole into "The Treasure" chamber, and here stand upright. Any further extensions of the cave are inaccessible. The once beautiful stalactites "clustering like grapes and acorns of frosted silver, or pendent from the roof like hugh icicles" are now broken down and candlesmoke has smeared the white stalagmitic incrustations".

Mr. J.D. Mason in the "Gentleman's Magazine" for May 1866 wrote:

"On reading the play of 'Cymbeline', I was particularly struck by the extraordinary coincidence that exists between the description of the cave which afforded a refuge to the wanderers, and that of a cavern near Tenby, Hoyle's Mouth".

Shakespeare makes Milford Haven partly the scene of Cymbeline, Act III, Scene II, where Imogen, hearing that Posthumus is there, enquires:
> 'How far is it
> to this same blessed Milford: and, by the way,
> Tell me how Wales was made so happy as
> To inherit such a haven:"

Milford is made the rendezvous of foreign invaders, where ambassadors embarked and landed. The cave would have been on the route taken by travellers from England to the Haven; it is in a hill, above "these flats" trodden by Belarius, and at the end of an overgrown path with neighbouring forest.

There is a local tradition that a passage runs from Hoyle's Mouth to the Wogan cave under Pembroke Castle, and that this passage was used as a secret way from Tenby to Pembroke in troubled times. A crack in the rear of the cave, which was a retreat of outlaws, was said to have the sea close behind it.

It was also said that a dog had once traversed the whole passage and "come out without a single hair on its body"; a visitor was said to have penetrated to "fine rooms"; it was the home of a wild boar, and finally that a commercial traveller, who had ventured inside, had never been seen again!

The Wogan, a "marvellous vault", a rocky cavern", is an almost circular excavated cave in solid limestone with a vaulted roof. Its maximum diameter is 76 ft 8 ins. and from east to west it measures 57 ft. 4 ins. It has a wide natural opening, which was built up to form a doorway and, in Elizabethan times, an account of this cave said that it contained a copious spring of water, which had ceased by the time Pembroke Castle surrendered to Cromwell. An adit, or opening, was said to be in the south-eastern corner of the cave, which communicated with Tenby.

Stabilisation work has recently taken place on one of Tenby's cliff faces. There is an old saying about the town:
> "Tenby will crumble
> Penally will drown
> St. Florence will become
> The new town".

Penally once used to be the favourite residence of St. Teilo, one of the most celebrated saints of the ancient British Church. He was born at Eglwys Gunniau, probably Gumfreston, near Tenby, became a schoolfellow of Saint David, and in AD.512 was consecrated Bishop of Llandaff.

He left Wales shortly afterwards because of the "yellow pestilence". This was caused by unburied bodies of the dead, which were left after a battle in the Hundred of Roos in Pembrokeshire.

St. Teilo answered a strange request, while living at his mansion in Penally. Legend says that, when Aircol Lawhir was King of Dyfed and held his court at Liscastle, he drank heavily every night, and as a result, one of the soldiers or family of the King was always killed. St. Teilo was ordered to come to bless the King and his court. He did this and sent two of his disciples to serve the court with meat and drink in moderation. No further murder was then committed and the King, freed of this danger, granted St. Teilo three villages, which seem to have been in the vale of St. Florence.

It is said that St. Teilo is buried at Penally, but there was a dispute between Llandaff, Llandilo and Penally as to which should have the privilege of his burial. After all night prayers, a miracle was performed, for the next morning three identical bodies were discovered, and he was buried in each parish. The Roman Catholic Church in Tenby is dedicated to him.

Town Walls from North West

22

Personalities

The "Tenby Observer" was established by Richard Mason in 1853, and was printed and published at the Library, High Street, Tenby. Richard Mason was born in 1817 and, after a dispute with his father over the improvements to the family farm in Hereford county, visited Tenby. He was so enchanted by the town, and his health improved so much, that he bought the business belonging to Mr. Hough of Jasperly House, High Street, a bookseller, printer and librarian. He brought his wife and child to Tenby, sold up his farm and in 1853 printed "The Tenby List of Visitors" which became in the second number, the "Tenby Observer".

Richard Mason published many fine literary works, including the six-volume second series of "Archaeologia Cambrensis". He also published Norris' "Etchings of the Architectural Antiquities of Tenby". and many guides to the town. He became a Councillor and Alderman, and received the thanks of the Queen for his services towards the erection of the Albert Memorial.

This memorial dominates Castle Hill above the Harbour, and the foundation stone was laid on the third anniversary of the death of the Prince Consort, December 14th 1864. The stone is a block of Pembrokeshire marble, and has a circular carving cut in it, which contains a hermetically sealed bottle. This holds a roll of vellum, bearing the date, names of the committee, and other particulars.

The statue itself is of Sicilian marble, upon a pedestal with four engraved panels. The left panel bears a shield charged with the Prince's hereditary arms, quartered with those of Her Majesty.

The right panel bears the shield with arms of the last native sovereign of Wales, Llewelyn ab Gruffydd, gules and or, four lions guardant counterchanged.

The panel behind the statue bears the monogram of the Queen and Prince Albert, with an escutcheon supported by the "Red Dragon of Cadwaladr". There is a recumbent leek and a scroll, inscribed: "Anorchfygol Ddraig Cymru", which means in translation from the Welsh: "The Dragon of Wales' is Invincible".

The front panel forms a tablet inscribed "Albert Dda, Priod Ein Gorhoffus Ffrenhines, Victoria", in translation: "Albert the Good, Consort of our beloved Queen, Victoria".

Richard Mason gives these details in his "Illustrated Guide to Tenby", and says that the memorial was inaugurated in the presence of His Royal Highness Prince Arthur and suite on Wednesday 2nd 1865. The number of people who subscribed to the Memorial Fund was about 16,500 and the total cost £2,250. The site was given by the late Reverend J. H. A. Philipps of Picton Castle.

Another memorial made in Tenby was the planting of two oak-trees in 1862 by the Mayor, Mr. George White. These were in honour of the Prince of Wales' wedding and are situated on the slope which leads to the Cemetery.

The "Tenby Observer" was owned in 1904 by Frank B. Mason, born 14th December 1856, who took over the paper at the age of twenty-five, and whose father had founded it as part of the family business of building, auctioneering and estate agency. When his chief reporter was absent in London, Frank B. Mason, who wrote a weekly column of criticism, under the name "Tatler", decided to report the Council Meeting on 21st January 1907 himself.

As a result of his report, which was described as inaccurate and insulting, he was banned from further meetings and an injunction was sought to this effect.

In November 1907, an action took place in the High Court, when the judge, Mr. Justice Kekewich ruled that meetings of Tenby Town Council were private and Frank B. Mason was restrained from attending them. Within twenty-four hours of his judgment, the judge died suddenly an operation. An appeal was lodged but later dismissed with costs.

The "Tenby Observer" considered it a great honour to have championed the rights of a free Press, and in 1908 published the text of the Local Authorities (Admission of the Press) Bill, which allowed reporters to attend the meetings of every local authority.

Frank B. Mason stood for the Council and was successful, his election according to the "Tenby Observer", nullifying the injunction against him.

After two years, the legal battle was won, with great expense to Frank B. Mason. The 1908 Act remained unchanged for fifty years, until it was extended under the Public Bodies Act of 1960.

The "Tenby Observer", which is Pembrokeshire's oldest newspaper, celebrated its 125th year of publication in 1978, when it received congratulations and greetings from the Queen and Prime Minister.

Charles Norris, the Tenby artist, was born in London, at Hughenden Manor, Bucks, in 1779. He was left an orphan with a considerable estate, and was educated at Eton and Oxford (Christ's College), but left without taking a degree. He obtained a commission in the King's Dragoon Guards. On September 25th 1800, he married Sarah Saunders, the daughter of a Norwich Congregational Minister. Norris was then 21 and Sarah 19. He resigned his commission and studied architecture, in order to pursue his career as an artist, and he settled in Tenby in 1805 or early 1806.

It is thought that Walter Savage Landor may have interested Norris in Tenby, for Landor had visited Tenby in 1795 at the time of his affair with "golden haired Nancy Jones". Norris planned to produce a work on mediaeval architecture.

Edward Laws says that "Norris sailed to Tenby with his family from Bristol on his yacht 'Nautilus'". In Tenby, he lived in an old house between Bridge Street and Crackwell Street, where there is a memorial tablet on the wall:

> Charles Norris 1779-1858
> Artist - Author of
> "Etchings of Tenby" 1812
> Lived here c.1805-1821

Seven years after he came to the town, he published forty plates of scenes in Tenby, which he drew and etched to illustrate the most striking features of Early Flemish Architecture. He made a complete record of the town's buildings of importance, except for the North Gate and the Whitesand Gate, which were both destroyed before he came to the town. His "Account of Tenby" and "Etchings of Tenby" can be seen in the Museum.

Seven children were born at Bridge Street, and three or four of them died, including Sarah, Mary and Ellen; in fact, eight of his eleven children died young, one of haemophilia. In October 1817, Tenby Corporation granted him a lease of a piece of land at Waterwynch for sixty years, or three lives. He undertook to spend at least £200 on building a house there within the next two years.

Norris's largest pictures are on exhibition in the Museum. Every aspect of the town in the nineteenth-century is shown in his work, which comprises more than three hundred drawings. He travelled all over Pembrokeshire sketching and filling portfolios, and visited Laugharne, Marros, Kidwelly, Worm's Head, Gower, Swansea, Cardiff, Chepstow, the Marches and Bristol.

His wife died at the age of 42. Some seventeen years after her death, he married his housekeeper, Elizabeth Harries, his junior by twenty-three years, and by whom he had three children.

Norris died at Waterwynch on October 16th 1858 aged 79 years. He was buried in Tenby cemetery, where his grave can be seen on top of a bank up some steps near the cemetery entrance. In 1879, his widow was laid in the same grave. His first wife and several of her children are buried in Penally churchyard.

Tenby is the birthplace of Augustus John, the artist, who was born here on January 4th 1878 in a large mauve house on the South Cliff. This house was then No 50, Rope Walk Field, and it looked out over the South Sands to Caldey Island and St. Margarets. His parents were staying in the town to avoid an epidemic of scarlet fever, which had broken out in Haverfordwest their home town.

After the death of Augustus' mother in 1873, his father and the young family moved to Tenby in 1874 and went to live in Victoria House, 32 Victoria Street, which was a nineteenth-century terraced house, with no sea view, behind Belgrave House. Augustus was christened Augustus Edwin John at St. Mary's Church, Tenby, on the 21st January 1886.

Sometimes the children stayed in Begelly, in a house which overlooked a gypsy community. The young schoolboy also explored Hoyle's Mouth Cave and roamed in The Burrows sand dunes. He was very fond of the harbour and also the long golden beaches, where he played with his brothers and sisters.

Augustus went to an infants' school in Victoria Street in 1884, then later to Greenhill School, which stood on the site of the present Public Library. The School has now moved to the outskirts of Tenby. In the grounds of Greenhill House, the original site, an oak tree has been planted in his memory, and a birch tree for his sister Gwen, also an artist.

He went on to boarding school at Clifton, Bristol, then in 1894 to the Slade School in London. In 1897, he went diving off Giltar Point, hitting his head on a submerged rock and had to have the wound stitched. He spent some time convalescing from his injury at Victoria House, and the subsequent change in his behaviour and his manner of painting, together with the rapid development of his work, gave rise to the legend that this accident made him a genius.

Augustus brought Dorelia, who appears in many of his pictures, to Tenby in 1920, to visit his father, who was convalescing from an operation on his nose.

The Freedom of the Borough was conferred on Augustus John, and his visit to receive this Freedom took place in October 1959. John, who was deeply moved, signed the Freeman's Roll, and at this time the audience in the Town Hall stood to sing "For he's a jolly good fellow". The "Tenby Observer" reported this event, commenting on the deep sincerity of the occasion.

He died on Tuesday, 31st October 1961, and was buried in Fordingbridge cemetery. A memorial service took place at St-Martin-in-the-Fields on January 12th 1962.

To celebrate the centenary of his birth, an Exhibition of his works was held at the National Museum of Wales in May 1978, which has a very large collection of his paintings and drawings.

Castle Gate

23

Exhibits, Shells and Collectors

The Reverend Gilbert Smith, Rector of Gumfreston, was a keen collector of geological and archaeological material, and he spent much time between 1840 and his death in 1879 digging in Hoyle's Mouth Cave, at Eel Point, Caldey, Black Rock Quarries, Penally, and at Coygan Cave, Llansadyrnin, Carmarthenshire. He found remains of prehistoric animals, and in 1860 read a paper on "The Bone Caves of Tenby", which was later published. The specimens he collected were arranged in glass cases and, when he died, his collection was expertly valued by a Cambridge Professor at £100.

In order to prevent the University of Cambridge from acquiring the collection, Mr. Charles Allen of 10, The Norton, Tenby subscribed £60 towards the purchase of the collection, and the remaining £40 was raised from dramatic entertainments. The first meeting of the Museum Committee met at Mr. Allen's house on the 14th January 1878, and the former National School Rooms on Castle Hill, adapted from part of Tenby Castle, were leased from Tenby Corporation. The Museum was officially opened on July 26th 1878 by Professor George Rolleston, M.D., F.R.S., from Oxford University.

In the Museum, Tenby Corporation's Charters and other civic records can be seen, also old maps of Pembrokeshire, and exhibits concerning the Old Victoria Pier, the Tenby railway, guns and military equipment. As well as rocks, fossils and seashore life, there are more than 600 pictures, many by local artists, summer visitors and residents, including those by

Norris and Augustus John. When space permits, prints, aquatints and engravings by Daniel and Sandby are shown, as well as works by other well-known artists.

Mr. Wilfred Harrison, who is also a historian and was formerly Deputy Headmaster of Greenhill School, has been Curator of the Museum since 1957. There have recently been many alterations, which include a refurnished Upper Gallery for the natural history collection, a new office and store-room for the old Tenby Borough Council records, and an extension for a new picture gallery.

The Museum celebrated its centenary in 1978, when great-grandchildren of the Reverend Gilbert Smith and Clr. Charles Allen were present as guests.

From the entrance, there is a magnificent view of the Castle Beach and the South Sands. These Sands are the "principal ground for the shell collector" as stated in the past in Mason's "Guide to Tenby":

"Beautiful molluscs used to be the speciality of the coast from Laugharne. Some thirty years ago, the late Mr. William Jenkins, for many years a well-known shell dealer in Tenby, discovered on a visit to the locality of Laugharne Sands a hundred fine specimens partially buried in fine sand at high water mark. These were wentletraps, scalaria turtonae and scalaria communis".

Tenby caves and rockpools supplied "an unrivalled variety of marine fauna - sea anemones, starfish, crabs". On the South Sands also, many shells were found among the refuse from boats, which used to dredge on the Caldey oyster beds. "A List of Shells found on the seashore at Tenby, Pembrokeshire", carefully handwritten by Captain Roberts, c.1849, is kept in the Museum Library.

Gosse, the marine biologist, spent much time in the area and wrote an elaborate work on sea anemones, "Actinologia Britannica (1858-60). He found that St. Catherine's caverns contained dogwinkle, the smooth anemone, snowy-disked anemone, acorn-shells, stag's-horn sponge, crumb-of-bread sponge, while on the north side grew barnacles, ascidia, which is a mollusc, mussels and scarlet and yellow sponges. The shallow entrance pools had fringed fronds of sweet oar-weed and dark-red dulse; starfishes were also present.

Above the South Beach, some fine teeth of the great cave bear were found on the Esplanade, while digging out a house foundation. These were in a small limestone fissure. Edward Laws discovered a mammoth's elbow joint at Tenby, and also peat from the sunken forest. A mammoth's humerus was also found at Amroth.

There are many references to the beauty of the coastline. Ernest Rhys said of the part of Saundersfoot round to St. Govan's and Stack Rocks, then on to Angle:

"...it is so notoriously picturesque, its rural neighbourhood is so verdurous and so becastled, that a dozen summers spent here need not exhaust its charm".

But it was Tenby's harbour that appealed to A. G. Bradley, who found it a charming place, with its leafy cliffs and the harbour protected by Castle Hill and St. Catherine's island. The sea was so clear and the climate pleasant, while the town's unusual character made it very well-known to people who came to visit it from other parts of the country.

Augustus John said there was nothing more beautiful to be found than unspoilt and restful Tenby, and George Owen of Henllys praised Tenby for its courteous and kind people.

Arthur Leach, a former Curator of Tenby Museum from 1940 to 1957, quotes the following passage from George Eliot's Journal:

"The air is delicious - soft but not sultry - and the sands and bathing such as are to be found nowhere else".

Mrs. S.C. Hall thought the town:

"One of the prettiest, pleasantest, and in all respects most attractive of the sea-bathing towns that adorn the coast of England and Wales", in her "Book of South Wales".

But perhaps the most unexpected reference to the town is given in "The Times" of October 28th 1857, when the reviewer of a book on the Bermudas "by a Field Officer" proposes:

"... if, one could completely re-model the Bermudas, they might be transformed into a watering-place as pleasant as Tenby or Scarborough".

Today, summer visitors throng the South Parade, where once Romans may have walked the cliff top of the "fine fortress on the broad ocean". Danes, Normans, Flemings have left their imprint upon this town which "stondeth on a main rokke, but not veri hy", with Caldey Island and St. Margaret's sheltering Tenby from the cold Atlantic breakers.

END